The Reluctant Mystic

The Reluctant Mystic

Autobiography of an Awakening

by Nancy Torgove Clasby

Printed in the United States of America
on SFI®-certified, acid-free paper.

Designed by Lisa Vega
Cover photo of author by Sue Riordan

ISBN 978-1-937650-70-4
Library of Congress Control Number 2016935521

493 South Pleasant Street
Amherst, Massachusetts 01002
413.230.3943
smallbatchbooks.com

To my three beautiful children, Misha, Erin, and Megan.
Thank you, Michael, for helping me bring them into my life.

Contents

I went to sleep one night and had the following dream: My life was a book. Each page was a full twenty-four hours. I started to read through the book one page at a time. All of a sudden, a huge gust of wind came up from behind me and blew all of the pages over, and I was left looking at the very end of the story.

My story had ended and I didn't have a chance to read the whole book. I realized in that moment that life is very short. I was upset that I hadn't had a chance to read my entire story. It was my story and I missed it. Pay attention to this moment. It's the only moment we have. Pay attention to this life. It's short.

Foreword

I put off writing this book for many years and for several reasons. For one, I was simply too busy raising my three children. But then my children grew up. For another, I was overwhelmed by the enormity of my experiences, worried that I wouldn't be able to do justice to the awakening that took my breath away all those years ago. But now I've had time to get used to my new life, and I'm no longer afraid to try to explain what happened, as honestly as I can.

And the third and perhaps biggest reason I've hesitated is that I am a skeptic by nature, and I know that if I were reading this book, I would be questioning virtually everything in it. How can we truly believe what we can't see with our naked eyes, what we can't hear with our own ears? But then I started thinking about eyeglasses and hearing aids, telescopes and microscopes, and all the other miracles of modern science that allow us to do things we once thought impossible, the mechanics of which most of us don't really understand and yet we believe, we *know*, exist. Leaves are whipped around in a frenzy by something that we can't see but that we know is the wind. The feeling I have when I think of a loved one—I can't see or hear that feeling, but I know it exists, and we call it love.

In 1996, I had an out-of-body experience that left me with an understanding of the universe and how we are all bound by unconditional love. This, in turn, led to my becoming a healer, and I have since helped hundreds of people deal with cancer and other life-threatening diseases.

In that moment, I was given the gift of grace, an internal spiritual awareness of generosity, compassion, forgiveness, and joy that transcended anything I had ever felt before. It was given to me generously, with great loving kindness. I had no idea what was to come, but I felt an overwhelming responsibility to do something with this gift. I thought, "Why me? What did I do to deserve this? How could I share with others what I had so freely been given?"

I had no idea that I would be given the privilege of helping people going through various stages of cancer or those confronting life's big questions: Is there something greater out there than what our five senses experience? Where was I before I was born and where do I go after this life? What is truly important in my present life?

Noel, my friend and an editor, suggested I write down some of my story, some of my visions and healings that I experienced with cancer patients. "It could make a great book, movie, or play," he said. With his encouragement, I wrote the stories down, not to convince anyone of their validity, but with the hope that if I could help even one person find peace or comfort and understanding in something much greater than him- or herself, it would be well worth the effort.

I was still hesitant, though, to put any of this in a book because it could make me sound like I am someone who is not grounded, sane, pragmatic, skeptical, or sensible. I am all of these things! The story sounds like someone who is given to flights of fancy, someone who has delusional thinking. It doesn't sound like solid thinking.

I don't want people to think of me as a crazy person. I do want them to take from the book the greatest teaching of all—that we are all connected by something so much greater and that we are here to be expressions of unconditional love. Once people start reading about second sight, how will they be able to trust all the other really important things that I am writing about?

For the people who are ready and want to hear it, the whole story will make sense. Others might think it's hogwash and say, "Come on, lady! Do you really expect me to believe this?" Maybe they'll think I'm making the whole story up. And that is okay.

My spiritual teachers told me that it would be very important for me to go about my work quietly and humbly. My mentor and confidant Reverend Patricia Long warned me, saying "Your light is turned way up." I needed to be careful not to blind others with it. "People only take in as much as they can," she said, "no matter how much is being given out. If you want them to walk in the light, you need to let them first feel it at the spiritual level that *they* are on. Once they start to feel grace, they may or may not choose or be ready to ask about it or even receive it." Everyone has the right to think and feel whatever rings true to them. Take what you like and leave the rest behind.

It is extremely important for me to emphasize that this book is not about me, my personality, or my ego. It is about the profound peace that is available to all of us if we pay attention to the still, inner voice within. For some reason still unbeknownst to me, I have the incredible privilege of channeling a small slice of what I felt when I left my body that day many years ago.

Up until that moment, I was a happy mother, bringing up three fast-growing children with all the pleasures and pressures that brings. I was very busy, but I was not unusual. Well, maybe I was a bit unusual. After all, my grandmother did call me on the phone when I was three years old, from heaven.

CHAPTER

1

AN ORDINARY MOTHER

When people asked me as a little girl what I wanted to be, I knew immediately and with great certainty that I would be very happy being a mother. I spent my teenage years working with children and eventually received a degree in early childhood special education from Lesley University in Cambridge, Massachusetts. I worked as a teacher until a few weeks before I gave birth to my first child. I was always happy in a classroom with all those children. In many ways, I had to use a lot of intuition in my classrooms.

I had been married three years when I conceived my first child. I knew upon the moment of conception that I was pregnant, as I saw the light of my son's spirit enter my womb. I took a pregnancy test soon after conception just to make sure. My vision was correct, and I had my first child about ten months later. The day I gave birth to my big, beautiful baby boy was the second best day of my life (the first was my wedding). The first time I looked into his eyes, I knew him from the inside out. We had been together many lifetimes and I knew he would be a tremendous source of love, joy, and fun. He was, and still is, my wise child. My friends used to call him my Buddha baby when he was little because he had a depth and understanding to him that was enormous.

I conceived a second time when my son was about two years old. I was still quite tired with a two-year-old at home. Within three months of that conception, I went to bed one night and had a nightmare that a black hand came to me and reached into my womb and took that spirit with it. I woke up the next morning and knew I had miscarried. I started to bleed later that morning and wound up in the doctor's office to find out that there was no longer a heartbeat inside of me. I was devastated.

However, I did conceive a third time and had a gorgeous, healthy baby girl. Once again, when I looked into her eyes, I knew we had been together in many lifetimes. She felt like home to me. She was, and still is, my courageous and strong child.

This was the third best day of my life. I felt like the spirit that had been taken away from me came back to see me again. Perhaps she knew that I was too tired to be with her the first time around. I felt incredibly blessed, joyful, and extremely busy.

When my first two children were old enough to sit up independently, I kept having a vision of a third little spirit sitting with them in the bathtub. This sweet little spirit only showed up at bath time. She looked like an effervescent vibration in the outline of a little child. The light that surrounded her included all the colors of the rainbow and had a gentle, lilting pulsation around it. It was clear to me that although I had had extremely difficult pregnancies, there would be a third spirit joining us.

She was born when my second child was three years old. I had all three of my children by Cesarean birth, and when I had my two daughters, after the anesthesia started to work, I saw many of my dead female ancestors come into the operating room and stand by the side of the table. They were all there—my two grandmothers, Lily and Goldah, my two aunts, Eleanor and Lucille, and one of the greatest lights in my life, Alice. Alice was a woman who took care of me and my brother and sister when we were children. She had the softest brown skin, a big belly laugh, and a deep voice that sounded like caramel. She taught me the meaning of unconditional love.

I could feel all of these women, stroking my hair and face. I knew they were there to soothe and protect me and the little female spirits that were coming through me. It was as though they were there to make sure that these baby girls had a safe entry into the world. I was really happy to see them.

When my second daughter was born, I had the same feeling when I looked into her eyes as I did when I saw my first two children for the first time. I felt an inner peace. I knew her from the inside out. She was, and is, my sweet, free-spirited child. This was the fourth best day of my life. When she was born, I knew in my heart that we were all here, that my family was complete. I felt incredibly blessed to be with all three of these beautiful spirits again.

CHAPTER 2
THE AWAKENING

Throughout my life, I have struggled with back pain. It began just before my thirteenth birthday, and I spent the next four years taking painkillers. I couldn't sit down for long periods of time without unbearable pain, and for years, I ate standing up at a counter in my parents' kitchen. There were long periods of time when I couldn't go to school. I couldn't run, play soccer or softball, or take physical education in school.

The only way the doctor could see what was going on was through surgery, which I couldn't have until I was sixteen, when I had stopped growing. When the doctor opened me up, he found an enormous ruptured disc in my low back—he said it looked like what you would find in a man who had been digging ditches his whole life.

The surgery was a big help, but the pain still comes back from time to time. Over the years I've learned how to manage and treat the pain. I learned early on that I could manage my life with much greater ease if I learned how to take care of myself. When I was eighteen years old, I started a gentle yoga practice, which I have continued for the past forty years. I also started seeing an acupuncturist, as well as a chiropractor and massage therapist, and I have continued these therapies off and on throughout my life.

When I was thirty-eight, my condition worsened, and I began a course of treatment with my acupuncturist, Barbara Ferro, and a new massage therapist I thought might help.

I had first gone to see Barbara in 1996, when she was new in town, and we became fast friends. Barbara helped me tremendously with my migraines, and she later helped my children with them as well. She is deeply spiritual, and has a very commanding presence—she always reminded me of the Wizard of Oz. She has been a healer and mentor to

Acupuncturist Barbara Ferro

many and was to become an important link to what I would eventually achieve in my own healing practice.

One day during that course of treatment for my back pain, I went into Barbara's office crying and told her that something horrible was going to happen. I explained that the back of my head felt like it was on fire—that there was tremendous pain and heat there—but it felt like it was someone else's pain. I didn't know whose it was, but I knew it wasn't mine. With the pain came a huge sadness.

The following week, my sister-in-law fell off her horse, hit her head, and died the next day from the blow. When I heard the news, I knew immediately that it had been my sister-in-law's pain that I felt in Barbara's office that day. It was an extremely tragic time in my family's life.

On a subsequent visit, I told Barbara that I was feeling energy running up my spine. I would later find out that was the beginning of the intuitive energy waking up inside of me. Much later, I found out that the energy I was feeling was called Kundalini energy in the Hindu tradition, which is the energy that expanded into the experience of a spontaneous awakening.

At the end of six weeks of getting a lot of acupuncture and massage, I went to see the massage therapist one more time. That was the day that changed everything.

I was on the table, fully clothed, and he was working at my head. All of a sudden, my body started to shake, and it felt like I left my body. My eyes were wide open, so I could see the room I was in, but I could also see through what I later found out was my "third eye," which is an invisible energy center everyone has that sits in the middle of the forehead and is the seat of intuition.

The experience I was having is beyond the limits of language, but I will do my best to explain it. I was having what I now know was an out-of-body (spontaneous awakening) transcendent experience. I saw two visions going on: I saw the physical world with my naked eyes, and I saw a vision that was like watching a movie inside my head. The movie was an incredible, all-encompassing light. It was everywhere, inside of me and outside of me. I was in it and it was in me. It took my breath away. It was so brilliant that I could not look at it full on. It was everything and nothing all at once. It was all-knowing, all-loving. It was all-powerful, but not at all scary. I felt completely accepted and loved. I felt as though I was truly "home."

As my body was shaking, I reached up and put my hands on the massage therapist's hands, and I said, "Can you feel that?" He had no idea what I was talking about. He was not experiencing what I was. It felt like the whole world was shaking, inside me and all around me. It felt like bliss—perfect peace. This light was pouring through me, and as it was pouring through me, it was teaching me things. My consciousness had expanded out beyond the confines of space and time.

In the vision, I couldn't actually see my body on the table; it was as if my body had melted. The whole physical world melted away, and I could only see the light. But at the same time, in my physical body, when I had my eyes open, I knew I was lying on the table—I could see the tin ceiling, which is still there today.

I have always believed that everything happens for a reason, even when we cannot comprehend why. How can we make sense of losing a baby to cancer, or the unbearable pain of genocide? The answers to these questions are outside of our intellectual understanding. But when I left my body that day, the entire universe made sense to me. I understood that there is a Divine order to everything, even the things we cannot understand with our human minds.

What I felt inside of me that day was blissful. It was an expanded experience of creation happening inside me and all around me. We see that same energy in the universe all the time when the seasons change, when the tides go in and out, when the night sky changes, when the moon waxes and wanes. Creation is the expansions and contractions in our lives, changing everything all around us. I was awestruck, grateful, and humbled by the magnitude of my awakening.

I also learned in that place that everything is possible. Our egos, our personalities, and our minds normally confine us to what is and what is not. During my out-of-body experience, everything was and everything was not, all at once. I felt one with everything, and yet I was still me. I had an inner knowing and sureness that everything is exactly the way it is supposed to be.

I felt all of humanity in those vibrations, and I knew from the inside out that we are all connected. I understood the truth of being alive in a human body and all that our lives present us. On that day I felt an unconditional, all-encompassing, all-knowing love. This love was so enormous that it blew apart the physical world. It melted everything.

Time seemed suspended while I was in that altered state on the massage table. Looking back, however, it must have lasted about forty-five minutes. When the session was over and I had to get up off the table, I looked into the therapist's eyes, and it felt like I was swimming inside his spirit. It was as if in that moment I was instantaneously merged with something enormous. I had embraced a much broader and greater aspect of love that did not contain the popular ideas of sexual attraction between two people but rather an all-encompassing, unconditional love for all of creation. This love was outside of attachments and the preconditioning that society often imposes. The therapist had no idea what had happened.

When I finally got up, I was stunned by what I had just experienced. I felt like I had died and a new version of me was born. I had to sit for a long time in the waiting room while the therapist took in another client.

I couldn't move. It was as though everything I had ever known in my life had changed in that forty-five minutes.

I knew this was the biggest moment in my life—bigger than anything I could imagine, even bigger than holding my precious babies for the first time, which for me was as close as I got to heaven on earth. But intellectually, I didn't know what had happened. My lifelong beliefs were stretched beyond any sense of what was once normal for me.

When I got to my car, I had to sit in it for an hour because I couldn't figure out how to put the key into the ignition or how to put my hands on the steering wheel. I suddenly felt like I was swimming in a sea of molasses. My body felt light and clear as a bell, but the world around me looked and felt heavy, thick, and lugubrious. My mind had dissolved into another frequency, and I was trying to operate here on earth in a much denser frequency. Perhaps it is similar to what astronauts feel when they come back into Earth's gravity.

I don't know how I got home—eventually I must have figured it out—but I do know that as I was driving there, the whole world was bathed in sparkling, brilliant turquoise light. I didn't feel confused, and there was nothing scary about it. I had been taken to—and remained at—another level of consciousness. As I drove home I noticed that I could see invisible energy fields around all living things—what I later found out are commonly called auras.

Watching different people as I drove home, I could see these energy fields around them, and I could understand their interactions. It was like being in a Disney movie. Some of the people were in love—they had big, puffy pink clouds around them. Around others I could see anger and fear—their energy fields were small and very constricted. I was completely awake and alive in the present moment. It was like living in another dimension.

Back home, I was pulled back into my family life. My children at the time were ages three, six, and nine. Surrounded by all the comforts of home, it took me a while to learn how to handle things.

I remember hearing the phone ring and thinking, "Okay, I hear that. How do I get my hand over to that thing and answer it?" It felt like I could put my hands through the phone—and other things as well. It felt like I could even walk through walls! I'd go to pick up the phone, and it felt like there was nothing there. I couldn't figure out how to handle it. I had a hard time in general maneuvering in the physical world.

What moved through me on that day was of unspeakable magnitude. In fact, I didn't speak about it for a long time, for at least six months. I didn't know what to say. It wasn't that I was worried about what other people would think of me if I told them, I just couldn't come up with the words. It was an intense experience with no language in it.

It was similar to when I was three years old and my grandma Goldah died. Soon after her death, I have a clear memory of hearing the phone ring. It was a big, heavy, black, old-fashioned rotary phone. I remember how smooth it felt in my small hands. She simply told me that she was okay and not to worry about her. She told me that she loved me and then hung up. I never told anyone about it because it seemed so natural to me that she would contact me. In retrospect, I have had many other transcendent experiences in my life, but I had difficulty communicating my experiences using language and I also didn't feel the need to—they all felt organically normal.

I don't know if my family noticed anything in the days and weeks after my awakening. I don't know if they even noticed that I wasn't eating. After all, I spent my time in the kitchen feeding three young children—I rarely sat down to a meal even when I did start eating again.

I was in such a heightened state that I didn't eat or sleep for three months. When I put something in my mouth and tried to chew and swallow it, it wouldn't go down my throat. I couldn't get anything down, and I had no appetite. It felt like all the energy was coming from the base of my spine and moving up through my body and popping out the top of my head. It felt like I was being fed by whatever you want to call that interconnectedness of life.

The less I ate, the higher I got. The lighter I got, the more connected I got to divinity. Many spiritual traditions use fasting as a way to get closer to whatever they call that higher energy. But I had no prior knowledge of this—it just happened all on its own.

I lost maybe five or ten pounds—nothing very noticeable—yet people would say, "Wow!" when they saw me. They noticed something. They would stop me and say, "Nancy, you look great. How are you feeling, what have you been doing?" They noticed I was different but they didn't know what it was. *I* know that what they were seeing was the light coming through my skin and my eyes. Ecstasy poured through me and sustained me.

A few years later I read about people who are "breatharians," who live with no intake or sustenance but rely solely on air, or what is called "pranic light." They live on the energy that comes from something greater than themselves. There are historical, documented cases of people living like that for many years. For me, it lasted about three months. At the time, I didn't question it. I was in a place of total acceptance.

I know that this all sounds unreal. But how could I make something up that I didn't even know was a possibility? I really didn't want anything to do with any of it. I didn't ask for it, and I wasn't looking for it. I was just trying to be a good mother, wife, daughter, sister, and friend. I was truly a reluctant mystic.

Eventually I realized the full magnitude of what was happening. I noticed that I could hear the phone ring before it rang, or I would see something happen in my mind's eye and then it would happen. Simple things, like seeing a glass of juice spill. Or I might hear a song in my head and it would come on the radio. It was as though I was in tune with a sound frequency few others can hear.

I had gained clairvoyance, which means "clear vision" and refers to the ability to gain information through means other than the known senses and often before something happens. I also had clairsentience, which is the ability to feel things before they happen, and clairaudience, the ability to hear things before they happen. These abilities are also called "second sight" and "knowings." I could sense everyday things happening just before they occurred, as though I was simultaneously in the future and the present. This makes sense to me now because I now know I had expanded outside the box of space and time that we live in. But initially, this was hard for even me to believe in.

About six months after my awakening, I turned on the television—something very rare for me—and what happened next was like a cosmic joke.

The 1946 Tyrone Power movie *The Razor's Edge* was on, and in the clip I saw, Tyrone Power was taken to the top of a mountain by a lama—a spiritual master or teacher. When the lama came back to get him, Power launched into a monologue on how he went to this place of complete perfection. When he was there he wanted to stay, but something was pulling him back. As he described his experience, I thought, "That's what happened to me!" I completely identified with Tyrone Power's monologue. This was my aha moment. As soon as I heard it, I burst into tears, sitting on the side of my bed.

I turned the television off and called David Meyer, a rabbi and family friend. I told him I needed to talk about something and asked if I could come see him. We set up an appointment—I think he might have even seen me that day.

When I told him what had happened to me, he was very calm and collected. He had a great poker face. He said, "Well, I'm going to have to get back to you, Nancy. Let me call you tomorrow." He talks about it all later in the book. He told me he was very surprised and a bit unnerved to hear somebody say that something like that had happened to them. He has since said that he had his doubts at first, but he never expressed that to me at the time and gave me nothing but his full support.

Rabbi Meyer told me that if I had been born in biblical times, people probably would have described me as a mystic—someone with second sight or somebody who dreams for people or heals people. But here I was, born in the twentieth century, living in a quiet New England town where everyone is focused on their children, jobs, boats, and houses. I thought, "Okay, God, really? What is it that you want from me?"

David had to dig deep—most of his time was spent tending to his daily flock, not with people coming to talk to him about mystical experiences. But he gave me enough language so that I could go to the library and get books on mysticism.

I started poring through the books, and to my amazement, I barely had to read them. All I had to do was put my hands on them, and the information flew off the pages and into my heart as though I had written the words myself.

In truth, I was connected to the superhighway of consciousness. It felt like I was watching movies 24/7 in my head of things that exist in the more subtle levels of consciousness that we can't see with our naked eyes.

CHAPTER

3

SECOND SIGHT

Some days I see a bright blue spot floating in my vision: it is the picture of my soul. I can't conjure it up; it seems to appear of its own free will. Sometimes I see it when I close my eyes, but more often it appears when my eyes are open. A few times it's grown in size. When I first started to see it, I thought to myself, "What in the world is that?" I later discovered that a great spiritual teacher in India wrote an entire book about this marvel. Despite being the size of a sesame seed, it contains all the wisdom of the universe within itself.

Every time I see this iridescent spot, I feel filled with love. When the blue pearl appears, I know that what I'm seeing or thinking represents my highest, truest self. I have been waiting for it to speak to me in words—it never does. It just lets me know when I'm supposed to be paying close attention to my thoughts, words, and actions. I feel it alerting me to what is truly important.

In the months following the awakening, I was seeing, hearing, and sensing all kinds of supernatural experiences at all hours of the day and night. When I looked at people, I could see their lives, like halos around their heads—but very often what I saw were little things, like what kind of car they drove, what their house looked like, and who was in their family. I felt like I was intruding on their lives, and I didn't know what to do with all of the information that was being fed to me.

I called these "knowings" because there wasn't a shred of doubt in me. I knew now that there was a universal intelligence that breathes life into every creation. I now had a direct, personal relationship with my creator. That powerful presence is always accessible and available to me. I just knew things that were impossible for me to know, sometimes because I had no normal knowledge of it and sometimes because they hadn't happened yet.

One time, I saw a friend of mine, in my mind's eye, and her car was tilted up off the ground, being towed by a truck. Later on—I don't remember what the time lapse was—I came around the corner and saw that friend's car hooked up to a tow truck, just as I had seen in my mind's eye.

I would hear, see, or feel something in my mind, and then in the physical world, I would hear it, see it, or feel it. Knowings kept pouring through me—when I was doing laundry, while at the grocery store. . . . It could be overwhelming. I kept thinking, "Why me?" I remember one time when I was bringing a load of laundry up the stairs, and little children's socks were falling all over the stairs, I sat down and started to cry, completely overwhelmed. I remember calling out to God, "Are you kidding me? Could you please pick someone else? I am too busy to be dealing with this right now!"

The knowings must have been poured into me when I left my body that day and came through me as I moved through my life, my relationships, and my experiences. Some of them were insignificant, like the ones I just mentioned, but others were much bigger, like knowing when someone was going to die or if someone was going to get healthy again. I never told anyone that they were going to die, even if I felt certain of it, because

I am not God. I would never want to take away someone's hope.

Then there were the knowings that brought me to tears, like when I would walk into a house of worship and put my hands on ancient texts. It felt like all the words in these books poured through me. The vibrations in churches, synagogues, and temples moved through me and brought me to my knees as joy, sadness, fear, love, grief, and relief bubbled up inside of me.

I could see the physical world that everyone sees with their eyes, but also the energetic world that exists in the more subtle realms of consciousness. I could see the emotional moods of people surrounding their physical bodies represented by the size, color, and texture of the energy fields around them. The "clouds" I was seeing around people, I learned, were their auras—the life-giving energy that sustains our bodies. People having a hard time were surrounded by dark clouds, just like the saying goes—you have a dark cloud hanging over your head. Joy, conversely, surrounded people with a bright white light containing all the colors of the rainbow.

I could see/sense these energy fields around all living things. The trees had enormous energy fields around them, wrapping around every single leaf and branch. I could see the energy vibrating around them. In the grocery store, I could see energy fields around all the fruits and vegetables. I could tell the difference between a healthy organic apple with a big bright aura and one that had been sprayed with pesticides and had almost no aura.

When we take into our bodies something that is healthy, it adds to our own life force. Thus the saying "you are what you eat." The concept works the same way with the people we surround ourselves with. When I am with people who are physically, emotionally, and spiritually healthy, I leave feeling great.

On the other hand, if I am with people who are sick on any level, if I am not careful, I come away from them feeling drained of my energy.

It's important for me to have clear energetic boundaries around myself if I am surrounded by sick people so that I don't become a trash receptacle for their garbage. Everyone has been around someone that feels like an emotional vampire, sucking all the energy out of you. When you leave them, you feel depleted and exhausted. The flip side is that when you are around someone who is clear as a bell with lots of healthy energy, you walk away from them feeling great.

I've learned that in order to keep my energy field healthy, it's important to surround myself with people whom I love and those who love me. Eating well, exercising, fresh air, and doing things that bring me joy are all aura builders.

When I was a little girl, I used to lie in bed at night and practice leaving my body and going to the ceiling of my bedroom to see what it felt like. I remember looking down on my body and thinking, "Wow! This is really cool. I can see things differently from up here." I never told anyone about it because it never dawned on me to share it. It was just something that I did to amuse myself if I couldn't fall asleep. I don't even know what made me think of doing it in the first place.

Today I know that this is called astral projection, which is the act of closing your eyes and inviting your spirit to move outside of your physical body. It is also called remote viewing. There are many well-documented cases of this when people have near-death experiences. After they come back to life, they are able to tell exactly what their loved ones were saying down the hall from their hospital rooms.

I used astral projection one time as an adult after my awakening while I was working as a healer. A woman came to see me and wanted to know about her daughter who lived in Arizona. She asked me to visit her daughter energetically to see how she was doing out there. While the woman was on the healing table, I sat down with my hands on the back of her head and closed my eyes. I left my body and went to her daughter's house in Arizona. After the healing, I described everything to her and told her what was going on with her daughter. I was spot-on in my description of her daughter's home and situation. I remember going in through the front door and looking around her house. Her daughter was doing great; she wasn't physically ill and her emotional state seemed healthy as well. Her mother just wanted to know how she was doing.

For a long time it was just so much fun being out of my body. I practiced this a lot as a teenager, when I was in physical pain from my backaches. I learned how to leave the pain behind.

Sometimes, meditation can open the door to second sight experiences. Not everyone who meditates receives access to this; I don't know how I got it. For months after my awakening, I lived in a constant meditative state where I was hyperaware of everything that was going on around me on many different levels of consciousness. I was completely mesmerized with the present world, minute by minute, all around me. It felt like I had completely merged with nature and all living creatures.

Sometimes it felt like I was experiencing the world around me in slow motion. I couldn't believe there was so much life inside of me and all around me and wondered how I could have missed this experience for most of my life. I felt incredibly alive, alert, and awake. Everything was extremely intense and magnified.

Living in a meditative, expanded state was wonderful in many ways. I could feel nature all around me. I remember standing in the middle of a circle of enormous pine trees and feeling the energy coming from them into me, coming from them into each other. I felt their connection to the earth. It was so overwhelming, it made me cry.

I could intuit the feelings of plants, birds, and flowers. Today I can still hear plants talking to me. It is torture for me to go to a plant nursery or garden center, as all of the plants are begging me to take them home and place them in the earth before they die! I can still look into the eyes of a squirrel or a chipmunk and understand this life force energy that some people call God is everywhere.

When I left my body that day during the awakening, I went to a place that has many dimensions—dimensions that we can't necessarily see, feel, or hear. That energy is called by many names. I hesitate to use just the one word, God, to describe that energy because many people don't have positive associations with religious institutions. I do believe, however, that every religion began with some ordinary person just like me, sitting on the side of a mountain or out in nature, who had a spiritual experience that allowed them to have a recognition that all of creation is sacredly connected. For me it was on a massage table. Their awakening unfolded inside them, representing something so much greater than anything they could really explain using a spoken language.

My awakening taught me that all religions lead people to the top of the same mountain. Each religious institution has its own set of rules and regulations on how to climb the mountain, but in the end, we are all climbing the same mountain.

The heart of my out-of-body experience was spiritual in nature in that it taught me that we are all here to give and receive unconditional love, and that is our only purpose here on earth. We all get to do that in our own unique way. Each of us has a gift, and our purpose is to reconnect with that gift and then give it away.

CHAPTER

4

THREE WISE TEACHERS

After the awakening, there I was with the universe pouring through me and no language to describe it and no one to share it with. I was looking for some concrete answers—I wasn't worried, just insatiably curious about what was happening to me and what I was supposed to do with this great gift I had been given.

I found out later that some people who have awakenings are hospitalized for mental illness, when in truth they are simply overwhelmed by the enormity of their experience and are unable to use language to describe it. I was lucky to find people who understood me, and no one ever questioned my sanity.

Three amazing people presented themselves to me at the perfect time and in the perfect way. That was to change my life—and those of many others—as they helped me on the path to where I am today.

I will be forever grateful to Rabbi David Meyer, Reverend Patricia Long, and Dr. Badri Rickhi for helping me put the pieces of my puzzle together. Here, they explain in their own words what their journeys with me were like.

Rabbi David Meyer

Rabbi David Meyer had absolutely no idea what I wanted to talk to him about when I called and asked to speak to him that day in 1998, after seeing Tyrone Power's monologue in the *The Razor's Edge*. The rabbi and I took a walk outside, and I poured my heart out for the first time about what had happened to me. He was the first person I had spoken to, and he listened patiently as I tried to explain. He was kind, clear, and open-minded, and he told me I was not crazy. Not once did he make me feel silly or uncomfortable about my retelling of the awakening. When I had finished talking, he told me that he would do some research and get back to me. He called me the next day and asked me to meet him at his office.

Reflections of Rabbi David Meyer

I had never had a similar conversation with anyone prior to that—nor have I since. She was coming to me as her rabbi and also as a friend—our families have been close for many years. I took counsel from another rabbi, who I felt could give me some direction and someone who was more attuned to the ways of a mystic than I am. My colleague affirmed that my response and direction were appropriate for Nancy. I think it's fair to say that her initial response to the experience was being shaken up. In fact, my first thoughts about it were in reference to a very famous biblical story.

In the book of Genesis, Jacob falls asleep in the desert and dreams about a ladder connecting heaven and earth. In the dream, he sees angels going up and down. God is revealed at the top of the ladder and says to Jacob, "You are not a fraud. The covenant that I established with your father and grandfather, you are a part of that and your descendants are part of that. It is going to be okay." At that time, Jacob was fleeing from his twin brother, who had promised to kill him.

Aside from that dream and the similarity to Nancy's having an awareness in a semiconscious state, the Bible says that Jacob woke up and he was shaken. I once read an article interpreting that biblical story that indicated that for those who have a mystical experience, the initial response is a feeling of being quite rattled, even fearful.

I immediately had a sense of grounding Nancy through the biblical tradition. I understood her to have had a mystical experience. I said to her that there are many eels in the ocean and some of them are electric. These can generate a big electrical shock. I said that because, frankly, I have never had a mystical experience. I've had some wondrous experiences—I have felt God's presence in my life both in terms of support, encouragement, and incredible blessings, but I have not had the mystical experience or witnessed the layering of reality the way Nancy had.

Did I ever doubt her? Sure! A little bit. I think that's fair. I also have enough of the skeptic in me that would encourage that. Did I ever express that to Nancy? I don't think so. I felt that I really needed to help provide support and guidance at a time that was clearly a life-changing moment.

I needed to help Nancy find someone who could speak the language of her experience better than I could. And Dr. Badri Rickhi, the Calgary-based psychiatrist, was the guy. Although her experience wasn't something that I could personally relate to, as her rabbi and friend I wanted to make sure that she didn't go floating away. There was some caution in all that I gave her. But caution wasn't the predominant message. The main message was for her to see what was being given to her and to explore it, and to talk to people. It's easier to understand it now than it was then. It was new and unusual for everyone at that time, including me. Again, it's not an area of Jewish tradition that I have personally pursued. I am a fairly conservative, mainstream kind of a guy. But I am open to the possibilities.

As far as her abilities to see and know things outside of the physical world, according to Judaism, prophecy, or the ability to see the future, is one of the goals of some forms of Jewish mysticism. One of my favorite prayers that I am doing at Friday night services is a little poem that goes like this:

Entrances to holiness are everywhere.
The possibility of ascent is all the time.
Even at unlikely times and unlikely places, there is no place on earth without the Presence.

I do believe that the world is filled with entrances to holiness if we are open to them—if we have a mind-set to experience that. I don't think that you have to have a mystical journey to experience that.

Today, I would say that I absolutely believe the things Nancy told me. Later on I myself took an hour to receive some healing energy from her, back in April of 2002. I was just coming off of some sabbatical time, and it was a chance for Nancy to help me re-enter back into my work mode and transition back into it with some balance. I have definitely sent some clients her way over the years. I think that Nancy's work is genuine.

* * *

After my life-changing experience, I was eager to add to my support system and help put my newfound abilities to good use. After two intense discussions with Rabbi David Meyer, friends suggested I contact Patricia Long, a former nun, who was at that time a minister at a local church. I called her to ask if we could meet to talk—I didn't tell her what it was about. She didn't ask what religion I was and agreed to meet me.

At that first meeting, I told her what had happened to me. In those days, I couldn't get through a conversation about my experience without weeping—tears of joy. It must have been quite disconcerting. Patricia asked me to come back to see her weekly, and she invited me to take part in my first-ever healing session. Unbeknownst to me, she had privately decided I was a mystic. Our conversation was to go on for years.

Reflections of Reverend Patricia Long

What I remember from that first meeting was Nancy asking me, "Why is this happening to me? I am a housewife with three little kids. Am I going crazy? Is this normal? Even if it is God, why did God pick me? And what *is* this that I am experiencing?"

There was a lot of hesitancy—a feeling of maybe receiving a gift she didn't want. She wasn't waiting for it, and she certainly didn't want this to go down as a mental illness. Yet when Nancy told me the actual story of the experience itself, her demeanor was the exact opposite—she was calm and confident. I got the feeling that this was real, this was healing, this was a gift that she was actually free to accept or reject.

I remember sensing that I did not want to make any decisions for her but I didn't want her walking too quickly down the path of, "Why is this happening to me? This shouldn't be happening to me. Is this normal? I don't want this." I didn't want her to go and just bury it before she really looked at it. I also remember saying to my husband, who was a monsignor in the Catholic Church for thirty-five years (before we got married), "George, of course I can't be sure, but I think I met a mystic today." He certainly knew what I was talking about. He just nodded his head.

I knew this was real because of the way Nancy described the experience without letting fear or her judgment interfere with it. She was quite in tune with my understanding of mysticism from the 1500s and mystics like St. Teresa of Ávila, John

Reverend Patricia Long

of the Cross, and other mystics that I learned about and whose writings I read when I was a young sister in the Church. It is a very strong part of my spirituality. From a very young age, I just always believed that God, or however you want to describe that entity, is in communion with us and not far away.

Over the years, I would say that I have been in the presence of only a few people who have a very thin veil separating them from what I would name as the Divine.

Nancy and a friend, a former Catholic priest who also became a minister, are the only people I know who've put flesh on those bones. Nancy absolutely has something that I don't have. I have no hesitation in saying that, particularly as the years go on and she has accepted and developed a gift of healing not only emotional and spiritual wounds, but time and again physical wounds. I suspected this would probably happen.

One of the first things I asked her to do was a presentation to a study group at my church. I introduced her as a young mystic. My husband was the chair of that committee that year and I ran it by him first. I said to him, "Let's have Nancy come in and just tell her story and allow people to ask questions and make comments." I knew this was all new for her, and that's when I told her the light doesn't only shine and give you an open path to direct you in, it can also blind like the sun. It's the beautiful sunshine that can also burn. I was very protective of her. I didn't want this new rosebud to be thrown out into the snow and killed. But I was also confident that when God gives a gift, or you can say it in a different way, when the student is ready, the teacher appears.

I think that the most important thing that can come of this book is that from the beginning of time, there has always been a yearning and a longing to experience the Divine. People think it's so separate from humanity, and above humanity, and beyond human gifts and talents and experiences. I hope this book says that there is love falling from the sky. And it is there for us to receive.

When I asked Nancy to join my church's healing group, her very first response was, "Wow, you want me to join you in this? Sure!"

The most important thing that Nancy does is that she reveals the multilayered reality of healing. Even if her clients don't physically heal, she allows people to come into their own and experience an intensity of life and love that had they not had this sickness and lived to be 100, they would have missed. They would have never experienced life at its best and its fullest. They are not saying they are happy [the sickness] happened; they are only saying they would have missed life and love and healing and being fully alive.

What is next for Nancy? I think it is to continue to accept how her gifts of healing work and to stay out of her own way and let the gift work.

Nancy's most remarkable achievements are her three beautiful children. That is how she first introduced herself to me. As she said, "I am a mother and only a mother. Why is this happening to me? Motherhood was enough. I could never have imagined the rest."

* * *

Few experts are held in higher regard in the world of spirituality and psychiatry than Badri Rickhi, of the University of Calgary. In 2009, he shared the $250,000 Dr. Rogers Prize, the largest prize in the world for complementary and alternative medicine.

A published researcher who lectures internationally, he is director of the Canadian Institute of Natural and Integrative Medicine, where he holds the position of research chair. He has been an appointed adviser to Health Canada on complementary therapies and was a past collaborator with the World Health Organization.

And he was Rabbi David Meyer's choice to guide me on my journey to becoming a "reluctant mystic." It turned out to be an inspired choice—my conversation with Dr. Rickhi has been ongoing for many years.

Reflections of Dr. Badri Rickhi

To be able to share in Nancy's experience really makes me feel the wonder of the whole universe and consciousness that is available to us all. My first connection with Nancy was a phone call from her rabbi. He told me that there was a woman in his congregation who had a spiritual experience but was having difficulty understanding it. He had sought advice from another rabbi but thought I might have something to offer. Could I help? I wasn't sure, but I would certainly try.

It was a very short conversation in between me seeing two patients. The rabbi didn't give me a lot of information about Nancy at that point. She called me soon after and we spoke at length. That was when I first heard her whole story. I was excited, as it gave me a chance to help someone explore her spirituality on a very deep level.

Dr. Badri Rickhi

Oddly, it felt very familiar to me. It was like hearing different pieces of the same puzzle that I had dealt with in my psychiatric practice. I was able to reframe it through a process that was appropriate for her. It was less intellectual and more of an intuitive process.

As she described it, there was within me an internal understanding. She would tell me her experiences, and I could feed them back to her. I helped her put words to her experiences. We began to build a stronger picture of the whole thing.

There was something taking place inside Nancy that was reorganizing her own psyche and allowing her to be more grounded about what had happened. I tried to help create psychological boundaries for her and give her a sense of peace.

The next part of our conversation was about watching her unfold into the experience and see where the universe was going to take her. It's like a wave—you ride the wave and see where it takes you. What happens with people who are having spiritual experiences is different for each individual. Some might become clairaudient, where they hear sounds and beautiful things. Others might become clairvoyant—they get visual appearances. For others it might be their sense of smell that becomes enhanced.

For Nancy, what I did was validate and explain to her how I understood those experiences. I tried to help her create a more stable platform for her to work from and see which direction the universe would take her—rather than lead her in any specific direction.

There were many telephone conversations; we didn't meet in person until quite a bit later. It was nice to have a face-to-face connection, but I think the connection was always there.

I felt that Nancy was having a genuine mystical experience. Many people have what I call pseudo-spiritual experiences: It is quite clear that it is coming from their intellect. But that was not Nancy. I never had any doubt about her mystical experience. One of the things you find out about those who are having true mystical experiences is that it is very difficult for them to understand the whole thing. If I get someone in my office telling me that they opened their heart center and then their crown center, I think, "Oh, here we go again!"

Some people will come and tell me that they are having something that feels like a mystical experience but they can make no sense out of it. Those are the people who go through the experience first and then the understanding comes after. Those people have wisdom rather than knowledge.

Nancy once told me that she had a dream where she was surrounded by women of all colors, ages, and sizes. She was sitting on a three-legged stool in the middle of their circle, and they were chanting around her. The legs on the stool represented strength and balance. I asked her if they broke the stool—she told me that the stool did break. I told her that it was a mystical initiation for her.

I have trained myself not to predict outcomes and instead let the direction flow. When Nancy later mentioned that she was thinking of becoming a healer, I said, "Okay, if that is where you need to go, then go there." Throughout Nancy's evolution, there were different paths that she could take. At one point we thought she might choose remote viewing, which I explained was the process of visualizing people, places, or things at a great distance. The U.S. military had tried this at one point. Nancy said, "I knew I could do that, but I had never heard the term before."

I recommended Nancy's work to a patient of mine who had terminal cancer in his spine. That patient sent her a round-trip airplane ticket to come from Boston to Calgary to work with him; this was her first trip to Calgary. She was only with us for a few days. She saw this man three or four times. He later died from his disease. Nancy came to my clinic with me and worked on several people who were sick with various diseases. The only thing I told her was to make sure that she looked after herself properly because the healer hardly ever spends time healing herself. I got a phone call one day from a physician named Dr. Scott. Nancy had seen one of her patients who had more or less been written off—she was going to die from cancer. After the patient saw Nancy over a month, she went back to the see the physician, and there was no cancer. The physician had asked Nancy to explain it, but Nancy passed it on to me. The physician phoned me and asked what happened. She wanted some sort of validation about Nancy's work. I was happy to give it to her.

Nancy's qualities are her simplicity, honesty, and her following the truth. When people get on a spiritual path, sometimes their whole life goes sideways. So many things change around you. People think that the spiritual path is this beatific ascension into some gorgeous afterlife. It isn't like that. Your whole life rearranges itself. You begin to face this journey, and it's a journey that is the life within yourself—but your whole culture and community outside change as well. So I would say that Nancy had to face this journey, which on one hand was so powerful and Divine, and yet on the other hand could be quite painful because all the attachments and the things we hold dear to us get challenged.

The journey is to go through that whole process and come through with some sense of equanimity and peaceful understanding of it. That is what Nancy has done and that is why I see her as a true mystic. The Divine does not discriminate. The Divine chooses whom the Divine chooses, and that person has really earned that, whether in this lifetime or a previous lifetime. Things don't happen by accident. We earn whatever merits the Divine gives us.

CHAPTER

5

MY PATH TO HEALING

I remember being nervous the first time I went to see Patricia Long. I walked into the office of the church, not knowing what to expect. The church secretary greeted me and then went in to get Patricia. Out walks this tiny lady with a huge smile, ready to offer me a big hug. I was immediately relaxed in her presence.

As one of my teachers, Patricia gave me books to read and had many stories to share with me. She was a powerhouse of information. She helped me identify and further clarify my knowings, dreams, and waking experiences through another lens. She was also very protective of me. She said she saw me like a new rosebud and didn't want me to be "thrown out into the snow and killed."

We began meeting weekly, and Patricia asked me to come to a healing service for her church's healing group. I didn't know what to expect, but I was excited to be working with Patricia.

When we arrived at her church on October 28, 1997, for the healing service, only one woman showed up. Her skin was yellowish and very parched. Her eyes were dark with worry, and I could see that her energy field was dark and constricted. She seemed to collapse into her chair. Patricia played peaceful music, and then we three closed our eyes and prayed. I immediately felt myself fill up with energy, but I didn't know what to expect next.

When I first put my hands on the woman, much to my surprise, I could see inside her body. It felt like a movie was playing inside my head. I was completely fascinated. The first thing I saw was a bright flash of red, the color of the woman's root energy center that sits at the base of the spine. At the time, I had no idea what I was seeing; I found out later that this is the energy center for survival.

Her torso looked like it was filled with a honeycomb—it was sticky and dripping with a substance that looked like honey. I was receiving clear, sparkling energy into the top of my head, which I could then transfer to her. I noticed that it was getting stuck in the honeycomb.

Next, I saw the color green in her heart center, which is in the middle of the chest. I believe this is the most important spot in the body because this is the place where we give and receive unconditional love, the single most important thing that we do on earth. I placed my hands on her chest and let my energy flow into her. Tears streamed down my cheeks as I felt energy pouring through me and out of me. I could visibly see the woman's body begin to relax and melt open. She remained still as she received the warming energy. She left that day with a much lighter step. I knew then that I would become a healer.

At my second healing session at the church, the same woman came back. There was no black cloud hanging around her head this time. She looked much better, lighter, like she was starting to become more transparent, as though she had started on her spiritual healing journey (which is not the same thing as being free of physical disease). It seemed as though the thought of letting go, surrendering to God's will, might not be as suffocating as she had felt the week before. I knew she would die soon. This time I saw her in my mind's eye with angel's wings, floating in the air. I knew she would find peace.

When I first started working with people as a healer, I would come home completely exhausted. I didn't know how to separate my energy from the energy of the people who were sick—there was a lot of unwanted toxic energy about. Sometimes, being empathic, I would use some of my own energy, which is much less efficient than that of the source. In order to protect myself from that, I learned to say a prayer of gratitude before and after each healing, and to wash my hands in cold water and take a moment to be still afterward. My friend Barbara also taught me to surround myself with white light before doing a healing and to cleanse myself energetically afterward.

Today I always wash my hands in cold water after a healing. Many years later and hundreds of healings later, I automatically take care of myself energetically around other people. I also think I have a bevy of angels that look after me.

My purpose is to help people heal, to help people awaken to who they truly are, for them to remember their goodness, their sense of humor, their kindness, their generosity—their own special skill set that they have been given. Not my skill set, but their skill set.

Because I had to deal with so much physical pain at such a young age, I had to learn about humility, patience, letting go, gratitude, and kindness. I taught myself how to move into the center of the pain and breathe through it. I found a still point deep within that moved me away from pain jail. My pain taught me how to be in the moment. It gave me a sense of compassion and empathy for others who are in tremendous pain.

When I am ready to do a healing, I go to an altered state of consciousness through breathing and prayer. That's when I reach the "space in between." I sometimes call this "the great pause of life." It's one of my favorite places to be. I find that sweet spot at the end of the "out" breath but before I begin the "in" breath. I can rest in it, in the space between my thoughts. I can hear it in the stillness of the air before a storm, sense it in the dawning of the day, as well as feel it in certain inverted yoga postures, where your feet are above your head. When I am upside down, it feels like there is a nectar flowing from my body through my neck that automatically switches off my thinking. With no thoughts, I can float in spaciousness and freedom. All thoughts cease and I am simply a part of everything that is. I find this space when I meditate, pray, or simply sit in silence. It's a place of deep peace, equanimity, serenity, and connection to something much greater than anything I could ever imagine. It feels like home to me.

Everyone, in fact, has the ability to tap into this quiet stillness, to intuit experiences and relationships in their lives. If we are paying attention, we can feel intuition in our physical bodies. It might show up as a tightness in the stomach or as a softening in the heart center. You just know.

My intuition comes automatically to me at different times. Sometimes when I have someone on the healing table, I can ask for guidance for the person on the table. After they have settled down for a deep rest, I simply ask silently, "Is there anything that you want me to see here that will be of benefit to the person on the table? Please show me."

If you are extremely close to someone, you can intuit how they are in any given moment. It's fairly simple to do if you hold someone close to your heart, even if you don't physically see them regularly. For me, it's usually the people in my inner circle who are easiest for me to check in with intuitively.

But I can sometimes intuit things for people who come to see me as well—although I am a lot more cautious now about what I share. Today, I no longer look or ask for intuitive guidance.

For a long time I could see the angel of death standing down at the right corner of my healing table, down by my client's right foot. The angel of death would come in preparation for someone who was getting ready to die. It was an incredibly brilliant spirit, enormous, neither male nor female, full of white light and not scary at all. It stayed at the base of the healing table for many months sometimes, patiently waiting for the person to be ready to cross over. I was never afraid when the angel of death was at the healing table.

But while it was great to sit in silence with the angel of death, I knew it wasn't up to me to tell the client that death was waiting. There was nothing I could do, nor was there anything I wanted to do to change someone else's fate. It was not up to me to intervene with the natural outcome of someone's life.

I had been seeing a patient for a long time, a wonderful man who was incredibly diligent about getting better. His deceased father would often visit us during healings, and said to me one day that his son was going to be okay. I told his son and his wife that after the healing, and they were of course overjoyed at the news. He wound up dying several months later and the whole family was devastated. His wife kept saying to me, "How could this happen? You said he was going to be okay. What happened?"

I felt incredibly responsible for perhaps leading them down a path that wasn't necessarily true. I felt horrible about the whole thing. Of course I know that death is never a consolation prize for "being okay." We are indeed "okay" when we transition out of our physical bodies—that must have been what his dad meant—but it was not the okay they were looking for. This experience helped me understand how careful I must be when I share information that I receive from my intuition. It's not always appropriate for me to share what I see with my clients because sometimes they don't want to know. Sometimes, they just want to come and rest.

I decided after that experience to step back from looking and listening with my second sight. It was too much pressure.

I've had some people come to me with photos of their loved ones who have died, and we will take a moment to look at them and then put them out on display during the healing. We intentionally call the spirits into the room with hands of light and hands of love. I did this once with a woman who came to see me after her mother died. We put photos of her mother all around the room, and the daughter even brought her mother's favorite sweater. The daughter got some great messages from her mother that day during the healing. She intuitively knew that her mother was present. She felt her mother's love for her and had a great sense of comfort about her mother's passing.

Just because someone has died doesn't mean that they are no longer available to us. The communication is simply in a different form. Sometimes you will see a loved one who has died in a beam of light coming in through the window or shining on the ocean, or you will receive a visit from them in a dream. Sometimes you will hear a loved one in a piece of music and sometimes you can even smell them in the air. Pay attention! They are everywhere trying to get you to notice them.

My intuition is so strong that it's difficult for me to go into secondhand or antiques shops because all of those items bring someone else's spirit with them. It's too confusing for me.

At first, having second sight was extremely fascinating, but as time went on, it became extremely distracting, confusing, and even distressing. Perhaps you can understand how living like that would be too much. I was often exhausted and would have to nap after healings.

As years went by, the second sight made it hard for me to live in the physical world. I began to feel overloaded with stimulation and information that I had access to—information I could do nothing with. I didn't want to be seeing spirits everywhere and know when someone was going to die. It was all too much for me to take in. In addition, people were always trying to test me, to see if I was for real or faking. Once I start pulling things out of what seems like my bag of magic, it detracts from the most important part of the message that I was given that day—that we are here to give and receive unconditional love, and we all do that in different ways. The skill set that seems magical can be extremely distracting because once people think you can do those magic tricks, that's all they want to see. They want to know if I can move objects across a table just by my thoughts or separate from my body to move elsewhere (astral projection), or if I can see through them.

Eventually, I asked for most of my second sight to be taken away, and much of what sounds magical has been removed for me, and I am grateful for that. I simply prayed for it to be removed and, gradually, it was. Can I get it back? I hope not. I can still tap into the intuitive part of my consciousness, and that is enough for me. Today, the simple joys of life far outweigh the intense highs that carried me through the first ten years after the awakening.

CHAPTER

6

SHARING MY GIFT

I think that most people come to see me because they are terrified of death. Many people come to me as a last-ditch effort when everything else they have tried has failed. Others come to see me when they are moving toward the end of their lives and are curious to know about the big picture. Through my internal experiences, I am able to share with them that life doesn't completely end as we know it when we drop our bodies.

Oftentimes in the past people came to see me for reassurance—they wanted to know what my take was on their state of health. Because of my second sight, I was able to look inside the body and see from a different perspective. I don't do that these days; there was too much pressure for me to get it right. Some people were staring death in the face and wanted to know if they were going to survive.

Yet I love working with people toward the end of their lives, because they are able to open up and allow the truth in. They have begun to let go of all the minutiae of everyday life and are sincerely interested in the big picture: What is my life about? What have I done with my life? Who am I? Where am I going?

I can help people with these answers because I had a chance to see a sliver of the truth the day I left my body. I have completely lost any shred of fear about dying and have deep belief in an afterlife. My truth is, it is impossible to extinguish the light that we see in people's eyes because that light goes on from here to eternity and back again. My truth is, we are here to give and receive unconditional love, and there are as many ways to do that as there are living creatures in the world.

Following are the stories of some of my clients, some who are still with us, and some who have passed away. I am incredibly grateful to all those who helped me fill in some of the missing pieces.

Linda LoConte

I began pouring clear, sparkling energy all around Linda's cancer to see if it would melt. It took several weeks, but the cancerous tumor finally melted away completely. Her doctors were astounded. So was I!

Linda was my first client. She had breast cancer, resulting in a single mastectomy and a regimen of oral chemotherapy for seven years. In November of 1997, she was diagnosed again with a metastasis of breast cancer in her liver.

A mutual acquaintance referred Linda to me, and we arranged to meet. That first Sunday morning we met, I went to her condominium overlooking the local harbor with a massage table that I borrowed from a friend. We set the healing table up in front of a long set of sliding glass doors. I went there every Sunday morning for more than a year.

When I first saw her, she had a cancerous growth on her liver that was so big, I could feel it with my hands. Every week I would sit looking out over the harbor with my hands on her liver. I could feel the heat coming out through the palms of my hands. We worked together, bathing, cleansing, and loving her liver. We brought lots of light into her. I could feel the cancerous growth melting under my hands like melting butter. Those healings were extremely powerful, as I was still in a very expanded state from my awakening.

I was definitely nervous before we started; I wasn't sure what to expect. But once we started working, the soft, loving energy filled me and I settled down. Linda fell into a deep state of relaxation within a few minutes.

The second time I worked on her, I asked to be shown by the spirit world if there was anything that I needed to see. I was completely amazed that I could see the cancer on her liver. I was definitely taken aback. In my mind's eye, I saw a cross section of her liver, which was soft, wet, and pink. Surrounding the liver was a green, sinewy substance. When I tried to remove it energetically, I discovered it was very hard and stubborn. I tried to scrape it off with an imagined rock-like form with no luck. Then I tried to cut it off with big, sharp scissors in my mind's eye. The cancerous tumor was stronger than anything I could find in the physical world. It also felt angry, hot, and cantankerous.

Then the idea of using the white light and unconditional love that I saw and felt on the day of my awakening suddenly popped into my head. In my imagination, I began pouring that clear, sparkling energy all around the cancer to see if it would melt. Instead of using aggression, which comes from fear, I tried surrounding it with love to soften it up. I asked Linda to join me in this pursuit through visualization.

It took several weeks, but the cancerous tumor finally melted away completely. Her doctors were astounded. So was I! Linda and I were so surprised that we hardly talked about the truth of the whole experience, almost as though if we said it out loud, the tumor would come back. We were overjoyed with the outcome of our prayers and healing visualizations. What we had accomplished was unheard of. The tumor had been very large and now it was gone completely.

Linda felt so much better that in April of that year, she took a trip of a lifetime to see the tulip fields blossom in Holland with her oldest son, Craig, who was twenty-five at the time. They had an unforgettable trip.

Linda stayed on a constant dose of oral chemotherapy. Later, she had her gallbladder out as a result of an infection that wouldn't heal. She was definitely weakened as a result of that surgery and the exhaustion from the previous cancers. In time, her cancer reemerged in her ovaries. She began to grow extremely weary.

We spent a lot of time together in prayer and meditation. We also spent a lot of time visualizing what it would be like for her to leave her body and move into the next level of consciousness. I took her to "heaven" many times. I'd move her into a state of deep relaxation and then bring her to a place in her mind's eye that was wide open. There are no closed doors or windows in this place—all is possible. There's a sense of complete freedom, spaciousness, deep knowing, and wisdom. When you are there, you are completely in the moment. I would invite her to rest and remember who she was . . . her generosity, her compassion, her humor, and her loving kindness.

One morning while I was working on her, I looked across the harbor, watching the wind blow. It was making ripples in the water and moving the treetops on the horizon. Then something very unusual happened. I saw everything come to a complete stop. No movement, no sound, nothing. It was like watching a movie and someone pressed pause. I couldn't believe my eyes. In my heart, I sensed the magnitude of this moment.

Somehow, I had found a portal and transcended to a place where there is no time, only one present moment. All of time was suspended.

Of course, as soon as my brain caught up with this experience, the experience closed down and life began moving again as before. It lasted only a few seconds, and yet I knew it was enormous. I sensed that I had caught a glimpse of a slice of the space where there is no time. I had to mull this over and let the perfection of the moment gel in my mind.

By Wednesday of that week, I was ready to talk to my teacher, Badri Rickhi, about all of this. He always seems to be able to take my "out-of-this-world" experiences and help organize them eloquently with human language.

Here is how he framed it for me: He said that what I saw was the nothingness of God. The universe gave me another gift. Time slowed down to show me that the universe is made up of things seen and unseen. What is seen is the manifested. Yet the other half of the universe is unseen, unmanifested. He used the stars as a great example of this.

When we look into the night sky, we only see the stars, and yet it's the space around the stars that energetically holds all the stars in place. It's these great voids that hold the entire universe together. I was privileged to see one of these great voids. When people meditate, they look for that nothingness inside. I got a chance to see how nothingness can manifest itself. Perfect healing exists in these pauses.

Most people watch the movie and ignore this nothingness. These voids are equally as important but much harder to come into contact with. When a healer works on a client, the healing energy flows down through them first. It has to move through the healer's energy filters first, and if these filters aren't clean, then the healer moves their own debris down from themselves and into the client. Even with the best of intentions, they can make matters worse for their client.

I know for many people this will be difficult to understand. Obviously, I am not talking about physical debris. Rather, I am speaking about energy, which can be clear as a bell like a newborn or sticky like someone who is very needy or dark and scary, like the boogeyman under your bed. The healer must become a great void so that energy can move smoothly and clearly to the client. That spot of emptiness becomes incredibly important if the healer wants to be effective.

Since I had experienced perfect love, I can call that energy into my body and filter it into my clients. When I start my healings, I ask that I be as clear as a hollow log for unconditional love to flow through me. I invite myself to rest in one of those great voids, and then I invite whoever is on my table to join me in that place of emptiness.

This is where all healing takes place. The mind shuts down, the silence moves in, and then everything is possible. What an incredible privilege it is to be able to rest in this place of deep peace and unconditional love and share it with someone in need.

I went to see Linda a few days before she died. She was heavily drugged and unconscious much of the time. But when I came into her room, she opened her eyes and motioned for me to come toward her bed. She spoke to me in a whisper and asked me to tell her once again where she was going. I told her with great sincerity and excitement that she was going to be very pleasantly surprised. I told her that she was safe, guarded, and guided. I told her to let go of her fear and, as corny as it may sound, to move toward the incredible light. I don't know if everyone's experience is the same, but I know that light exists for everyone, dead or alive. Linda closed her eyes once again, and I bid her a safe journey and told her how much I loved her. She was incredibly courageous.

The day before she passed away, her ninety-year-old dad, Joseph Scott, came to visit her from Philadelphia. Her two sons thought they might have to carry him up the flight of stairs that led into her condominium, but he made the climb all by himself. Linda had been completely unconscious due to being heavily medicated and at death's door. However, the minute her father entered her room, she sat up in her bed and they talked for a few hours. She was totally lucid. She died twelve hours later.

Dr. Angela O'Brien

"Nancy helped me heal emotionally. . . . She was particularly attuned to my suffering, my vulnerabilities, and my fears about not being able to conceive. She saw right through all of my bravado and busyness."

Dr. Angela O'Brien has been a chiropractor for thirty years and has helped me for many years. She runs an extremely busy practice and travels all over the country teaching and lecturing.

When I first had the awakening, it was hard for me to shut off the knowings pouring through me. I couldn't stop them. Everywhere I turned I could see and feel other people's pain. I knew I could help many of them, but I had a lot of questions: Do I help everyone? Do I offer my help? Or do I stay back and wait until they come to me for help? I could sense things that hadn't even happened yet. What was I supposed to do with the bombardment of insights I was receiving? Most often, I waited until I was asked for help.

I was seeing Angela three or four times a week in those days because of my back pain, and our physical contact made it hard for me to ignore her suffering. Today, I choose not to look into other people's stuff the way I used to because it was all too overwhelming. However, if you are paying attention, so much is obvious.

Angela had been trying to get pregnant for four years. Sensing her stress level, I volunteered to meditate on what might be going on in her body.

"Nancy helped me heal emotionally at a time that I really needed help," Angela says. "She was particularly attuned to my suffering, my vulnerabilities, and my fears about not being able to conceive. She saw right through all of my bravado and busyness. The fast pace of my life kept me from really feeling all of my emotions around the forty-eight losses I had—one a month for four years. I had gotten to the point where I was feeling that I just wasn't going to be a mother.

"Nancy was able to get to the very core of what was going on with me. She gave me spiritual comfort in her certainty that I was going to be a mother and that I was going to have these two children. She was absolutely certain that I was going to be a mother of two. She was confident that her assessment was correct. That was very comforting because she gave me a lot of hope."

One of the things I could do was go inside other people's bodies. I would close my eyes and ask to be shown what I needed to know. We sat down together in a quiet place to meditate on her situation. I was shocked when I realized that I was inside her uterus. It doesn't make sense intellectually, but I intuitively knew what I was seeing. I sensed that all of her female organs were healthy, and Angela confirmed that—there was nothing wrong with her reproductive organs.

Later that afternoon I had a vision of her. It was a picture of her head, and on top of her head was an hourglass timer. On either side of the hourglass were two little angels. I wasn't sure what it meant at that point. Did it mean that she was running out of time? Or did it mean, be patient—your time will come?

A week later, I went for a walk with my youngest daughter to an old cemetery in our town. We were looking at headstones for a school project. On one of the headstones, I saw a picture of a woman. She had the same hourglass over her head and two little angels on either side of the hourglass.

I couldn't believe my eyes. A second confirmation. This time I knew that she would conceive two babies.

"I think Nancy is a lot more in tune than most," Angela says. "I believe that everyone has the capacity to be aware, and yet most people are too busy to notice or pay attention to it. Nancy is tapped into that universal consciousness that I believe we all share. When you combine that with her nurturing ways—all I can say is that you are lucky if you know her."

In time, Angela had two beautiful baby boys a few years apart—Aidan and Liam. Today I am truly blessed to be able to call Angela my friend. She has been very instrumental in keeping my back in good shape and has been a great role model for me as a hardworking and extremely competent chiropractor, a healer in her own right, and an amazing mother.

Ellen Kennedy

Ellen was one of the rare people who truly saw her cancer experience as a gift. She had a quiet, clear energy about her.

When Ellen Kennedy first came to see me, I immediately recognized her from around town. She stood at my door, tall and willowy, and her eyes told me that she was in the process of emotionally and spiritually transforming in large ways because of her diagnosis of third-stage breast cancer.

Several people had referred Ellen to me, including a hospice nurse who had been a client of mine for a long time and knew that Ellen was interested in alternative healing. Ellen was one of the rare people who truly saw her cancer experience as a gift. She had a quiet, clear energy about her. She was interested in exploring what was going on inside of her emotional/spiritual being as well as her physical being.

Ellen came to see me after she had had two surgeries to remove her breast cancer, but the oncologist wasn't sure she was cancer-free. She was going to continue doing her traditional therapies; however, she was interested in keeping the cancer from returning.

As we began a brief conversation, it was quite clear that she had done a lot of homework to learn about her disease. She was open-minded, available, and teachable. She still had her hair at that first meeting, before she went through eight rounds of chemotherapy, which was followed by radiation treatments.

During our first healing, which was all about appreciation and acceptance, I could see an outline of the cancer in her body—perhaps it was an energetic shadow of what had been there. I knew after that meeting that she would be okay with whatever came down her path.

When I first meet someone, I try to keep the conversations to a minimum. It's easier for me to do my work without a lot of verbal exchange. Sometimes the less I know, the easier it is for me to read someone's energy. I also find that many people get quite upset in the retelling of their story, and then it takes me the first twenty minutes of the healing to calm them down. I don't need to know all of the particulars of someone's life in order to connect with them on a higher plane.

The next time I saw Ellen, she told me about what happened to her when she went home after our first healing. She said she had a dream that night that she was still in my living room on my healing table. She was surprised that my busy household was going on all around her as she lay on the table. She said she could see and hear my children in the house with her. She had a feeling that she wanted to stay on the table forever.

At some point in the dream she got up and went into the bathroom at my house, and she said she got the sense that there was a huge purging of her toxicity. All of a sudden she saw a very bright light coming out of the toilet. I can just imagine what you are thinking at this point in her story. When she woke up, she knew she would be healed by our work together and that she had come to the right place.

Since I am not a talking therapist, very often it takes a long time for me to get to know about my clients' everyday lives. However, it takes me only one session to feel the energy inside and around the client. Ellen's energy was open, soft, wise, and tender. She allowed me to use all sorts of healing techniques with her.

When I first started working with her, I was simply using the laying on of hands, as well as prayer and guided visualizations. Through the years I learned various energy techniques, and Ellen allowed me to use all of my new tools on her. I taught her the prayer for loving kindness, worked with crystals, told her healing stories, used my polarity, reiki, craniosacral therapy, and reflexology.

We used color for chakra clearing, worked on her breathing, did emotional clearing, read articles on meditation, and worked with positive affirmations. I told her my healing dreams, taught her restorative yoga, helped her with grief and loss, cleaned her organs from the inside out, taught her about letting go of self-judgment, and used relaxation techniques. Throughout all of this, she remained open and enthusiastic about her growth. I saw her blossom into an even greater version of who she already was when she first came to see me.

It's important to understand that I never do the healing myself; I lead people to a place of deep peace where healing is available to them. I would never be so presumptuous to believe that I could heal anyone myself—I believe it is the energy that pours through me that does the healing. When people come to see me there is always a healing of a spiritual nature, and sometimes a physical healing occurs as well.

It was wonderful to see Ellen grow in health—a healthy mind, healthy heart, healthy body, and healthy spirit. She has had no return of any cancer cells in her body. She worked very hard to be in charge of her own healing process. I was merely a witness to her journey.

"I feel very strongly that the treatment I received from Nancy made a huge difference in my life," Ellen says. "I attribute my recovery to her and how she spoke to me. What she said to me calmed me down mentally and gave me a chance to get well physically. If Nancy had been a different type of person, the healings might not have helped me as much. It was more about her and what she was doing than the techniques themselves. I felt deeply connected to Nancy on many levels. If the connection had not been there, I feel that I would not have healed as quickly."

I am truly grateful to still be a part of Ellen's life and to share with her all that I've learned on my journey.

Dr. Arthur Freedman

The prognosis was fair—not good, but fair. They gave him a 40 to 60 percent chance of getting through it, of surviving. "I have been free from melanoma for eight years now. . . . I do believe Nancy's work has helped."

Arthur Freedman is a successful and busy veterinarian. His dealings with cancer started after a mole that had been removed from his groin was diagnosed as melanoma. The doctors had ignored it for a while, then it started to change in character. That was when Arthur said, "I want it out."

The pathology on the adjacent lymph nodes came back positive with melanoma. The prognosis was fair—not good, but fair. They gave him a 40 to 60 percent chance of getting through it, of surviving.

When he was diagnosed with cancer, his wife, Ellen Kennedy, said, "Please go see Nancy! I know you believe in this stuff. And look what it did for me." He saw me before and after his surgeries. I asked Ellen to come to the healing sessions with Arthur—I love to include my clients' loved ones in their healing process. I find that the healings are that much more powerful when the person on the table is surrounded by many loving hands.

Arthur believes stress plays a big part in a lot of cancers, and he thinks his stress level was up when he got the diagnosis. The doctors talked to Arthur about "five years"—they never talked about a cure. They recommended radiation therapy, modified chemotherapy, and interferon, an antiviral agent that fights tumors, which can make you quite sick. Since Arthur was holistically trained in homeopathy and believed in other modalities, he declined those treatments and instead continued with homeopathy, nutritional support, acupuncture, and seeing me.

There are a great many alternative remedies available that claim to work, if you look for them. Arthur didn't chase everything out there—he doesn't believe in taking twenty pills a day—but he has settled on a few things he believes helps. He tries to eat a mostly vegetarian diet and takes four supplements a day: curcumin, an anti-inflammatory that comes from turmeric and can help suppress some kinds of cancer growths; vitamin D; nutriferon, which is a supplement to help boost the immune system; and a Standard Process general concentrated vitamin, which is concentrated food that also has certain vitamins in it.

Arthur also goes to a melanoma support group—mainly to help new people now. He has sent clients as well as the people in his support group to me over the years.

"As far as my visits with Nancy, I feel relaxed when I'm there," Arthur says. "I have to rejoin the world quickly when I leave to return to my clinic and see patients. I do believe that my work with her helps to correct some of the energy within my body to try to better fight off any cancer. I think it helps my body better focus.

"I don't know if I'm rid of cancer until it comes back or I die. I have been free from melanoma for eight years now. I think all of the modalities

I chose came together and helped me heal. I do believe Nancy's work has helped. If I didn't, I wouldn't be coming to see her every week.

"My strongest recommendation is to seek alternative care, not just go for the chemotherapy, radiation, and the interferon. Energy medicine can help influence and support the body, to help stimulate it to help fight off the cancer. It helps emotionally as well as physically."

Arthur continues to get better and was able to return to riding in the Pan-Mass Challenge, a grueling cycling benefit. It has been an honor to know this incredibly intelligent and capable man. His resolve to do his healing his way showed me the meaning of courage.

Helen Hoch

"When I come to see Nancy, I feel very grounded. I have a lot of faith in her connection. I feel that she is the channel for me."

In almost forty years as a psychotherapist, Helen, a mother of two adult daughters, has dealt with everything from helping people deal with major mental illnesses to helping people adjust to life transitions.

In August of 2001, she went for a mammogram and was quite shocked to be told she had breast cancer. She had surgery, then chemotherapy, and finally, radiation.

"I was very sick when I first started seeing Nancy," Helen says, "because my immune system was compromised. I continued to see her regularly for the next ten years. I got cancer a second time in September

2011. I was even more surprised this time. It was the same kind of cancer, same breast, two different episodes of it. Their guess was that it wasn't a spread of the first cancer; it was just unlucky to have two occurrences of the same kind of cancer in the same place. The second time it was not as aggressive as the first time. I wound up having an almost nine-hour surgery with three surgeons.

"I was originally recommended to Nancy by two different massage therapists. I had a lot of faith in their recommendations and was open to the idea of seeing a healer. The first time I went to see her I remember feeling taken care of. . . . I suspended judgment. I felt a nice connection—warm and caring. I felt good enough to want to go back again. I went weekly for a very long time.

"After my chemotherapy, I was extremely sick and very compromised. By the time I got to the radiation, I was actually feeling better. I looked forward to our visits each week. I felt like it was me being taken care of by Nancy in this very spiritual way and it was also me taking care of myself. It was very empowering.

"When I come to see Nancy, I feel very grounded. I have a lot of faith in her connection. I feel that she is the channel for me. I am very spiritual, although not remotely religious. I think about health, healing, and spirits. I feel like she lines me up. She is like a direct line to God.

"I never stopped seeing Nancy all these years. I still see her every four or five weeks. After my last big surgery, Nancy came and picked me up for my appointments and brought me home because I couldn't drive. It felt good and gave me a sense of continuity and familiarity. I felt like I was back on my healing path again. It was a very important part of my healing process."

In all the years that Helen has been coming to see me, she has not been sick other than her two cancer diagnoses. She never had the flu or sore throats or even a cold in our harsh New England winters. I always tell her that she has a rock-solid constitution.

Helen thinks that my constant emphasis on gratitude is a tremendous reminder for her. It's so easy to fall into negative thinking, especially when faced with a life-threatening disease. She loves that my work is soothingly consistent. I try to use the same phrases from session to session. Moving from chaos into stillness is extremely healing. In some ways, our work is similar in that we are both healers and both empathetic and tuned in.

The first time I put my hands on Helen's heart center in the middle of her chest, I couldn't believe how beautiful and soft it was. It is one of the most gorgeous places to be in the whole world. It feels like whipped cream with sugar in it. I love sitting with her.

When Helen comes in to see me, she is full of energy and talks very quickly with great enthusiasm, and as soon as I put my hands on her, she is out in two seconds flat. She doesn't move a muscle or make a sound throughout the entire healing. She settles right down. It is always a privilege to be in silence with her.

Helen comes from a medical family with its fair share of skeptics. "My father was a doctor and my mother was a nurse," she says. "I have a lot of doctors in my extended family. I am not saying that Nancy's work has cured my cancer, but I can say that it really helps me through it. My father had passed away before I was diagnosed with cancer. I think if he had been alive, he might say, 'This is a little silly, Helen.' But he would never make me feel bad about it. My own oncologist never discouraged me from doing all this stuff. Even my oncological surgeon was supportive.

"I am very grateful that Nancy is in my life. I consider her as being part of an anchor that grounds me to this world. She keeps me optimistic and feeling like I am doing something proactive for myself."

Sharon Hynes

Sharon had tumors everywhere. She was terrified and angry. "After the healing, she was a completely different person," her mother, Helen, says. "She didn't have the terror after she saw Nancy. The trauma was gone."

I met Sharon through her sister Suzanne, an extraordinary landscape designer who had long helped me with my garden.

Sharon had orthopedic problems all her life, and had fifteen surgeries before she was eighteen years old. She hated doctors passionately, and for good reason.

A few years ago Sharon became very ill. A chiropractor friend of Suzanne's took X-rays of Sharon's neck and told her that she needed to go see her primary care doctor. At the time, she didn't have one. She got one the next day, and the doctor sent her to see an oncologist. She had tumors everywhere.

Sharon was to die only six weeks later.

Her mother, Helen, says, "Sharon was physically challenged all of her life. She was totally independent from the day she was born. You knew automatically when you were in her presence that she was in charge of herself.

"She was born in Alaska. My husband was stationed there in the military. When she was about a year old she needed a special surgery. The best place was at a hospital in Boston. In order for the military to pay for our flights there, she had to spend the night before we left in one of their facilities.

"When we came to get her the next morning, one of the young military men brought Sharon to the airport to meet us. She looked at me, then she looked at her father. Then she turned her head the other way with a look on her face that said, 'I am never going to forgive you for this one!' She was very aware from the get-go. She always had a way of expressing herself, even as a little girl."

Suzanne says about her sister: "It is very important to remember that Sharon always wanted to be treated just like everybody else. That was a challenge for her because of how other people viewed her. She went to a regular school all the way through high school."

Suzanne had been to visit my healing table many times throughout the years for shingles, and she really thought that her sister would benefit too. But Sharon resisted. "Sharon was going through very severe trauma when she first got sick," Suzanne says. "She was in a lot of spiritual and emotional pain. Just horrible, horrible pain. I kept telling her that I wanted her to go see Nancy because a session with her would be healing. I didn't even know in what way—I just knew it would help her. She was in such a traumatized place that she just wasn't able to go. But Nancy remained ever open and ever ready.

"I got a call from Sharon one day, and it was a very emotional phone call. She was telling me things that she would say if she thought she was going to die. I remember her saying 'I am such an asshole.' That was a life review for her. I told her that she was the most courageous person I had ever met. I said to her, 'Listen, I think now would be a perfect time for you to go see Nancy. Would you be open to that? We can go right now.

"She went silent. I said to her that I know her well enough to know that means yes and I would be there in five minutes. Meanwhile I was talking to Nancy on the phone as I drove to pick up Sharon. I said to Nancy in a panic, 'She's coming! She's coming! How is she going to get up your stairs? How will she get on your table?' And Nancy said to me, 'It will be just fine.'

"Well, my sister leapt up those stairs. No hand railing. The steps were high. I'm still shocked at the thought of how my sister did that. She practically vaulted onto the healing table from the little stool that Nancy had beside the table. The whole thing was amazing!"

Suzanne helped throughout the entire healing. It was a miraculous sight to see the two sisters together in such an intimate and powerful process. I kept whispering in Sharon's ear that she was indeed greatly loved exactly as she was by her creator and that she was perfect exactly as she was. She heard that. She was very dear.

Suzanne says, "That was her only visit to Nancy. The healing was so powerful that when she was done with the session, she gave Nancy a huge hug with an energy that I hadn't seen from her since she was an open-hearted, joyous little girl. I had never seen her respond to a stranger as openly as she responded to Nancy that day. She definitely did not like to be touched by anyone, and there she was on the table being touched ever so gently by myself and Nancy. Her heart just opened right up."

"Nancy had a calmness about her that helped Sharon greatly," Helen says. "After the healing, she was a completely different person. She still had severe physical pain and she went through a horrible, horrible dying process for six weeks. But she didn't have the terror after she saw Nancy. The trauma was gone.

"After the healing—for the very first time—she started to let us do things for her. Up until that point she would never let anyone do anything for her, *ever*! But she would do anything for you.

"After she saw Nancy, she had surrendered completely. She let us do everything for her. She even asked us to do things for her. Much to my amazement, she asked me to brush her hair and rub her legs. She asked me to sit where she could see me. She always wanted a hand over her heart center in the middle of her chest because that is what Nancy had done while she was on the healing table. She said that it helped her breathe. It was wonderful to see her like that. It had opened her up so much. She let us love her totally and completely, which she had never allowed before. It was a big gift to us that she let us take care of her."

Suzanne says, "When Sharon was dying, I talked to her about all the things Nancy had taught me. She knew and trusted her. I kept telling her to make sure that she moved toward the light. Just go right through to the light."

To be able to face death without fear, or with less fear, is miraculous. Sharon was an inspiration for us all.

Stan Atkins

Stan was dying of cancer at the age of eighty-one. They found a spot on his lung and it progressed really fast from there. "He had a great attitude," his daughter Meredith says. "He said that his number was up, [so] why not go along with it?"

Meredith, Stan's daughter, and I grew up in the same town. We met in our twenties before we had our children. We were pregnant at the same time, she with her first baby and me with my second.

"I knew that Nancy was working with cancer patients but I didn't understand the real power of her healings until she came to my father's house to help him at the end of his life," Meredith says.

Meredith's father was dying of cancer at the age of eighty-one. He had gone to the doctor for a pain in his arm, and that's when they found the spot on his lung. He was diagnosed with lung cancer, and it progressed really fast from there.

"He had a great attitude about it. He said to me that his number was up, [so] why not go along with it," says Meredith. "He had a few radiation treatments. He died six months after his diagnosis. He was born a Catholic and went to church every week. He was a firefighter, a positive person. He was a good soul and a great dad, an honest man, hardworking. He really cared about people. He would bring home the paycheck and my mother would give him five bucks. 'We would never have traveled or gone anywhere if I had been in charge of the finances,' he said."

I offered to help Meredith with a family healing for her dad. "I asked my mother if that would be something that they would like. They were sort of old fashioned, but both my mother and ailing father said, 'Sure!'" says Meredith.

I went to their house and set up my healing table in their living room. I put on some soft music, and we all stood around the table that Stan was lying on. We covered him with a soft blanket and put a pillow under his head. It was a bit difficult for him to move as he was very sick.

Meredith's youngest daughter, Hayley, was six at the time, and she had an amazing bond with her grandfather. Meredith and her family live right next door to her parents' home. Hayley sat at her grandfather's feet and held them throughout the healing. It was a great experience for her. Meredith's mom, Rebecca, sat at his head and placed her hands on his heart center. Meredith and her brother, Alan, stood on either side of their dad with their hands on his torso.

Meredith says, "I have another daughter, Chelsea, older than Hayley. She was in middle school at the time and was just as close to my father but couldn't be at the healing. I felt that my younger daughter coped with his death much easier than my older daughter. I attribute that to the healing circle and her experience of it.

"Nancy has a really soft, gentle voice that resonates quietly. It was a very comforting experience to know that you were involved with him moving on. It wasn't about us looking for a miracle."

I felt all this beautiful love coming out of everyone as I guided them through the healing. It gave them all a chance to express how they felt about him while he was still alive—something that sadly often happens only after the person dies.

"Sometimes, I think we have a lot of things backward," Meredith says. "Death is a natural part of life. When someone like Nancy comes along and gathers everyone together, we all feel like we are part of the process. You are getting a chance to send them through the next doorway."

Stan died on Father's Day in his home surrounded by those he loved.

Vincent Lique

He said his illnesses kept him on the edge of death at all times. He used the intensity of this to stay awake and mindful of his life moment by moment. He said it was a true gift to have to remember that life can be snatched away at any instant. He said he never wanted to be lulled into complacency.

For most of his life, Vincent Lique stared death in the face. At just nineteen, he was diagnosed with a very rare kidney disease and told he would not live past forty. New medicines, however, kept him healthy much longer. But by the age of fifty, he needed a kidney transplant. His brother stepped forward as the donor, and his gift gave Vincent back a tremendous amount of strength and energy.

But fate wasn't done with this father of two. A few years later he was diagnosed with kidney cancer—from the original kidney that was still in him. That was when Vincent first came to see me. This time, his doctors said he had eighteen months to live. In fact, he lived another three and a half years.

Vincent's kindness was far reaching. He adored his wife, Kathy, and their two daughters, Maya and Sara, who were both adopted from Korea. He served for twenty-five years as executive director of a program for the aged in Lynn, Massachusetts, where he helped a great many people.

I saw Vincent through the last three years of his life. One of the amazing things about him was that he really wanted to explore death and was always looking for people to talk to about it. He was very open-minded and curious about it—perhaps because he had been told at such a young age that he would die by the age of forty.

He said his illnesses kept him on the edge of death at all times. He used the intensity of this to stay awake and mindful of his life moment by moment. He said it was a true gift to have to remember that life can be snatched away at any instant. He said he never wanted to be lulled into complacency. Sometimes when he was feeling better, he would come in and say, "You know, Nance, I'm not sure I really want this cancer thing to go away because it's keeping me awake. I'm one of these guys who would sleepwalk through life if I could. But this experience of cancer means that I can't sleepwalk through anything."

Vincent told me that most people in his life felt unsettled and tentative about his impending departure. Because of my experience, I was able to share with him the enormous peace of the unimaginable, and he loved hearing about the next part of his journey and all that death brings. He soaked in everything that I told him with great vibrancy and alertness. He was not afraid to die.

We spent hours talking about the great pauses in life, the places of incredible stillness where we are deeply connected to that universal energy of creation. This stillness is what kept Vincent alive long enough to do some amazing traveling with his family during the last three years of his life.

He went rafting down the Grand Canyon with his wife and daughter Maya, and traveled to Italy, where his mother was from. He then decided that he wanted to find the place on earth that had the least amount of Western influence and came up with Bhutan. He fell in love with their concept of Gross National Happiness, with a real focus on human well-being.

Vincent would come to visit me every week between all his trips. His health was great throughout all of these adventures. Amazingly, he never felt the effects of his disease until three weeks before his death.

Vincent acquired another tumor—a metastasis of the kidney cancer—on the back of his head. His doctors convinced him to have some radiation on this tumor, as it was near his optic nerve and they were afraid it would impair his eyesight. Kathy believes that as a result of that radiation, with a compromised immune system, he contracted a very severe form of pneumonia. He was admitted to the hospital and got sicker and sicker.

Vincent had talked about dying often over the years, and he told Kathy that he didn't want to live if he was going to be really disabled. Finally, he was moved to the intensive care unit of a bigger city hospital. While he was there, he got another infection that would leave him with serious limitations if he lived through it.

After talking to Vincent's doctor about what his life would be like, Kathy knew that he wouldn't want to live with those limitations. The family agreed to take him off life support. Vincent was sixty-five.

"Nancy was one of his biggest supporters during the last three years of his life," Kathy says. "He felt supported by her in a way that he had never felt supported by anyone else in his life. She was able to be open around dying and to walk down that path with him. That was something that he wasn't able to find from other people.

"Nancy wasn't there for him necessarily to get better physically. It was more about helping him die with joy in his heart. He had worked through a lot of his feelings around his death. He never looked the other way. He faced it head-on. Finding someone that can also look at it that way and just be there for him—and with him—was a rare find. Quite a gift."

Trish Grzela

Trish has a photo of herself with a beautiful tattoo on her reconstructed breast. "I figured that if I was going to look in the mirror and see something that was different, it had better look good!"

Trish is an amazing hair stylist I've known since high school. I really got to know her when I started going to her salon fifteen years ago.

"I realized that Nancy had something I needed right after I was diagnosed with breast cancer," Trish says. "She looked at me with this gentle smile and said that she mostly worked with people who were in various stages of cancer. That was the beginning of our work together.

"I went through surgery, chemotherapy, and radiation. The reason I needed Nancy was because I needed to stay in touch with my holistic belief in my health. I don't know if I would have been able to save my life without the help of conventional medicine like the chemotherapy and radiation. But if I was going to torture myself with those procedures, I needed to be supported and grounded more holistically as well.

"I started seeing Nancy at her office one week after I started my chemotherapy. I didn't know what to expect when I went in there—just being in her presence alone made me more relaxed. I would fall asleep within five minutes of being on her table.

"When I walked into her healing room, I could feel my heart rate slow down. I could feel my chest soften. I knew that for an hour I could let go of all of my thoughts that were swirling around and the pressure of what I still had coming up in the future."

Trish is amazing. She runs at one hundred miles per hour all day long. For her to come to my office and lie down on my healing table and have everything stop was contrary to everything that she is. Every cell in her being wants to go, go, go!

Trish says, "I could hear Nancy's voice talking, and the next thing I knew, I would be waking up about an hour later. One time, I remember waking up two hours later. She just let me sleep. Falling asleep on her table is different from falling asleep at night when you get into your bed."

Trish would come into my office on the run, jump up on my table, and within minutes, she would be out flat for the hour and then some. If I have the time, I love to let my clients going through physically challenging times rest for a good half hour after the healing is over. It sort of seals in all the good energy.

"I remember having a hard time driving home from her office some days," Trish says. "I was in a fog afterward. My brain got to shut down completely. Nancy would have me think of my favorite colors and smells to get me to slow down. At that point my favorite smell was the smell of my son's breath. He was six at the time and everything about him made me feel love. To this day when I smell him, I go back to that peaceful place.

"I have recommended Nancy to many people," says Trish. "I strongly believe in her work. She gave me a sense of freedom. All of a sudden you are free of all the stress, the fear, and the pressure of what all of it means. When I walked into her office, I would give out a big sigh of relief."

Trish competed in a breast cancer survivors' beauty pageant and won. It wasn't about external beauty, but about how you delivered your story and how the story was received. In her funny, quirky little ways, she inspired a lot of people with her story.

As part of the pageant, she got to do a photo shoot with an amazing photographer, and one of the photos hangs in one of her salons. She put a beautiful tattoo on her reconstructed breast. "I figured that if I was going to look in the mirror and see something that was different, it had better look good!" she says.

Mishi Torgove

There were spirits all over the hospital lobby. A woman looked at me and said, "Are you okay? You look like you just saw a ghost." I couldn't make that story up—I am not that creative!

I got a phone call from my brother, Andy, who told me that his son, Mishi, was in the intensive care unit at a major hospital in Manhattan for his asthma. He was unable to breathe normally on his own. My nephew became part of our family when my brother and sister-in-law Joni adopted him from Romania when he was three years old. He is an open and very lovable person who immediately captured all of our hearts. When I heard how sick he was, I volunteered to go to New York City immediately so that I could help out while he was in the hospital.

I walked into the reception area of a very busy hospital, and when I looked up I was very surprised to see what looked like patients shuffling around the lobby in their hospital gowns and slippers. I thought, *How strange that they would let sick people walk around in the lobby with all the hospital visitors.* Then I looked a little bit more closely: their skin was ashen, and their eyes were dark and hollow. I immediately knew that these people were already dead, but they did not yet know they had died. They were spirits who were caught between this world and the next. For various reasons, they were still bound to the earth.

I made my way to the elevator around the corner, and there was a woman there waiting to get on. She turned to me and said, "Are you okay? You look like you just saw a ghost." I realized once again that the God of my understanding has a great sense of humor. I couldn't make that story up—I'm not that creative!

While I was in New York, I stayed with Mishi during the day and prayed with my hands on his feet and chest. A few years later, my sister-in-law Joni asked me again to do a healing on Mishi for his asthma.

That was an overwhelmingly powerful healing. It was Mother's Day, and he fell asleep very quickly on my table. At that point, the spirit that I sensed was his birth mother, who had come to ask me if she could use my hands to touch him. She told him how much she loved him—she wanted him to know about her love so that he could breathe more easily. She tried to blow her love back into his lungs.

Mishi woke up feeling a bit confused, but there was no asthma attack the next morning.

The Bank President

There is always someone on the other side waiting to help us cross over.

This story took place in the very early days of my work as a healer. I got the opportunity to work with a wonderful, truly gentle man who also happened to be the president of one of the local banks.

He had colon cancer and was given three months to live. He initially came to see me with his wife and we spent an hour talking about what I did and how I got to be a healer. I told him that I thought I could help. With his wife's prodding, he agreed to have me pay them a visit. He really stretched himself spiritually to accept the healing in this form. In those days, I was still going to people's homes. I took my table to their house once a week, and we set it up in their living room.

At the end of the three-month period, he was still alive and living his life to the fullest. He made a few trips with his wife to visit family members. He told me he had a friend who had been diagnosed on the same day as him with the same kind of cancer, and they were both supposed to die at the three-month mark. His friend died almost to the day that his doctors told him he would. I kept telling my client that everything is possible and that the doctors were making educated guesses but weren't always right. My client lived another nine months.

His wife and I had been doing healings on him throughout the year. In my mind's eye, I kept seeing a traditionally dressed, older Chinese couple that came to every single healing. They sat in the two formal chairs that flanked the fireplace in my client's living room.

At the end of every healing, his wife and I would go into the kitchen to wash our hands. One day when we went into the kitchen, I said to her, "You are not going to believe this, but I am just going to say it. I hesitate because it doesn't sound very rational; it doesn't sound like it's a very real possibility." I told her about the Chinese couple I was seeing every week. We decided at the time not to tell her husband about it because we thought it would be too much for his banker's intellect.

I got a phone call from his wife two weeks before he died. She said to me, "Nancy, you are not going to believe what happened!" She told me that her husband was heavily medicated and unconscious most of the time. She told me that she walked past his room and noticed that he was in his bed with his eyes closed and yet he was carrying on a conversation with someone even though there was no one in the room with him.

She went into the room and gently shook him and said, "Honey, who are you talking to?" She said he opened his eyes and looked right at her and said, "I am talking to this elderly Chinese couple. They are helping me get my affairs in order before I leave." And with that, he closed his eyes and went back into an unconscious state. His wife told me that she almost fell over when she heard him say that. She reiterated that she never spoke a word to him of what I had said about the Chinese couple.

This whole experience leads me to believe that there is always someone on the other side waiting to help us cross over. Sometimes it's someone we knew, who has already died. Sometimes, it's someone in the spirit world who has come specifically to help us cross over into the next level of consciousness.

A painting by Maria DiGangi, one of her favorites.

"Cancer can be very isolating. I still feel sometimes like I am in a glass cage and I can't reach anyone else because they haven't been through cancer. . . . What Nancy has taught me is the ability to see that the sun is shining right now and this moment is all I have."

For twenty-two years, Maria was a full-time professor at a community college, teaching fine arts, painting, printmaking, and watercolor. She is an amazing artist who bases her work on her love of nature and wildlife.

Maria had her first cancer diagnosis five years before we met. She was forty-one, in the prime of life and enjoying her career. It was early-stage breast cancer, she was told, which posed no risk to her life. In the ten years following that, she had three much more devastating cancers—yet today her doctors tell her she is disease-free.

Today, Maria is a walking miracle. She says, "I am still here in large part because of Nancy's work. I am quite certain of that."

That first breast cancer scare was followed five years later with a diagnosis of stage-three melanoma cancer on her forearm that had spread to her underarm lymph node. A dermatologist had told her what she had on her arm was "nothing." She told him she was worried about it because it was itching and growing. It took another seven months for her to get a correct diagnosis of melanoma. She was then told that she had at best a fifty-fifty chance of living another five years.

That was when she first came to see me. The bulk of the cancer cells had been removed from her arm, and someone from her melanoma cancer support group suggested we meet. My practice has always been by word of mouth—no advertising, just people helping other people. Simple and quiet.

Maria had no idea what to expect. Two more cancers were to come along, but Maria stayed with our healing sessions.

"My work with Nancy is fairly dramatic," she said, "in that I come to see her feeling empty, just empty of water. That is the best way that I can describe it. I leave her feeling as if I've had a long drink of water and I can breathe again. I try to hold on to it as long as I can, until the next visit. If I could, I would come every day, every week, but that's not possible. I try to remember what she's told me and I try to keep those thoughts in my head as long as possible."

Our first session was about gratitude. That might sound ridiculous considering where Maria was at that point in her life. However, gratitude is always available and gives the person practicing it a changed attitude, which in turn benefits the entire person—body, mind, and spirit. Her "homework" that week was to begin keeping a gratitude journal. Very often, the mind takes up its home in thoughts of negativity. Being mindful on a daily basis of what is positive helps soothe whatever is ailing you.

Maria still hesitates to put words to her story. But because of her respect for the work we have done together for the last five years, she is telling her story for the first time in the hope that it might help someone else.

Another breast cancer diagnosis came two years after the melanoma. This was in the opposite breast and was entirely new, not related to the previous cancers. She had surgery to remove it and then watched it come back throughout the entire breast. A year later, she had a bilateral mastectomy to treat her third cancer.

She said, "When you get cancer over and over again—and, mind you, these are brand-new cancers, not spreading from a previous cancer—you start to feel that you are in a very special category. I felt doomed. Why the lesson again?"

But her healing sessions with me continued, once a week. Today she still sees me once a month. Maria has been a vegetarian for thirty-one years, drinks no alcohol, doesn't do drugs or smoke cigarettes ever, exercises regularly, and generally takes good care of herself. She did, however, spend lots of time in the sun as a kid and endured many sunburns.

She had to deal with loved ones telling her that she should sue the dermatologist who misdiagnosed her. But the last thing she wanted in her life was more negativity. She was being tugged at from all directions, and she had to try to stay true to her nature, which is peaceful and loving.

Right now, there is no evidence of cancer in her body. She takes no medication but continues to visit her doctor regularly. In addition to coming to see me, Maria said something else that really helped her was talking to other people who had cancer or another life-threatening diagnosis—because they are the only fellow human beings she can really relate to.

Maria said, "Cancer can be very isolating. I still feel sometimes like I am in a glass cage and I can't reach anyone else because they haven't been through cancer. I can't connect unless it's someone very elderly or someone who has dealt with this. I can't connect with the freedom that others have."

I understand what Maria means. Having your mortality right in your face every moment of your life can be quite overwhelming. That is why mindfulness practices of living in the moment—one thought, one feeling, and one minute at a time—become vital. Why go into "what-if" land when we can enjoy what is right in front of us? We practice staying in the moment at every healing.

"Nancy has helped me stay in the moment," Maria said. "The problem with cancer for me is that I am always thinking, 'Is this headache here because the cancer is coming back? Is this pain in my hip the cancer coming back?'

"We don't spend a lot of time talking because Nancy is not a talking therapist, but there are many times that I've been here and Nancy will work with me while I am on her healing table through prayer, meditation, and visualizations about the exact issue I am dealing with that very day. I leave sometimes thinking, 'Nancy, thank you.' She is spot-on. How does she know these things? She centers me. I am living proof of her work."

What Maria doesn't know is that I am always being helped by my higher power, whatever you choose to call that. I don't even understand how it works. It's almost as though I have antennae that go up and I can intuit things I shouldn't be able to know because no one has told them to me. Sometimes it's clearer than others, but if I ask for help, it always shows up in some way. I know that it comes from something greater than me because I couldn't even imagine most of the stuff that comes through me or out of my mouth. That's how I know it's authentic.

For Maria, as it is for most of us, her visits to see me are about her remembering how wonderful she is in many ways. She is extremely caring, thoughtful, dependable, generous, and extremely spiritual. She believes in the mysteries of life as well as death.

Maria, who loves nature and has a menagerie of wildlife that she feeds in her backyard, took in a feral cat one December. She had been feeding him outdoors, and when the weather started to turn, she brought him into her home. The cat wouldn't let Maria near him, and so he stayed in a room all by himself for six months.

In April of the next year she was diagnosed with melanoma. She was treated in May and started on a very rigorous protocol of medication for the month of June. She was so sick from the medicine that she couldn't get out of bed for the entire month. The cat who had never come near her found his way to her bedroom, got up on the bed, walked toward her, curled up right beside her, and put his paws on her. He hasn't left her side since! It was like a light switch turned on in him. She told him that she saved him and now it's his turn to save her. His name is Tomo, which means friend in Japanese.

"What Nancy has taught me is the ability to see that the sun is shining right now and this moment is all I have. It comes through whenever I am on her healing table and it's a reminder for me. I would give everything else up, but I will keep seeing Nancy as long as I am able to, as long as she is willing! She taught me that out of that fifty-fifty chance, I could be part of the fifty percent that lives. I didn't see it that way in the beginning."

Sam Hoffman

Sam beat brain cancer. Now he is becoming a nurse. "I owe much to Nancy," he says. "She was—and is—my inspiration."

It was a very unwelcome sixteenth birthday present, as Sam Hoffman says today. Out in his kayak, he discovered his nose streaming with blood after he went swimming. He was sick with flu-like symptoms for a month, toward the end of which he was unable to keep down food or water. That was when his mom took him to the hospital.

An MRI showed that he had a brain tumor. He was rushed to a larger hospital, where he underwent a nine-hour surgery to remove the tumor. The doctor took an extra three hours to make sure that he got everything.

He needed no further surgery. Sam still sends this doctor a thank-you note every once in a while. However, he did undergo chemotherapy and full spine and head radiation.

Sam was really in a desperate state of mind after his diagnosis. There was a moment right before he went into surgery when he was looking out of his fifteenth-floor hospital window and thinking about how he might get over to the window and open it so that he could go right out of it.

During Sam's slow recovery while he was going through chemo and radiation, his parents suggested he come and see me for healing. (I was a childhood friend of Sam's father.) "That was one of the best things that ever happened," Sam says. "After my first visit to Nancy for a healing, I was asleep within thirty seconds. When I woke up, I had no idea where I was. I was totally blissed out. I actually had energy again, which was a novel experience. I, unlike everyone else who got treated with the same regimen that I had, was only nauseous about three times. Each time was when I had something containing sugar. Everyone else was in a constant state of nausea throughout their chemotherapy.

"The healings with Nancy played a crucial role in this. Having been in school to become a nurse myself, from a scientific perspective, I can't tell you this is what made the difference. I can tell you I did feel absolutely wonderful, and that feeling carried me through many days after the healing.

"I never got back to being my old self; however, I did get back to being a new me, which was for the best. It took me four years to feel truly healthy again."

Sam's visits to me continued weekly, and doctors continued to be astounded by how quickly he was healing and how well he did during his chemo and radiation.

"Before my cancer experience, I was planning to go down a research work trajectory," Sam says. "In a large part because of the compassion—the energy of personal care and spiritual connection—I am in school right now to become a family nurse practitioner. My goals are to work with cancer patients from diagnosis through wherever their path leads, to provide holistic care, and refer them to practitioners such as Nancy to provide that connection in order to allow people to have the benefits that I had."

Sam changed his career path so that he can give back what was given to him. He wants to blend science and spirituality.

"Humanity is a big part of the cure," says Sam. "I am very committed to improving the quality of life for patients while lowering costs. Compassion is part of a patient's treatment. What it can achieve for the patient is a great addition to our health-care system. Compassion research started in the past five years—the government is now putting millions into this.

"I owe much to Nancy. She was—and is—my inspiration."

Steve Welling

Steve's doctors at Dana-Farber Cancer Institute were amazed at just how calm and collected he was. Little did they know, he brought his meditation practice with him.

It was a stunning blow when Steve Welling, a popular bartender, and his wife, Brenda Sterner-Welling, a former flight attendant, learned that he had a sixteen-pound tumor in his torso. After the diagnosis, Brenda came home and went to sleep, only to be awakened in the middle of the night.

When she opened her eyes, she was startled by a form at the foot of her bed. She believes that she saw her guardian angel. She got a message from her angel that everything was going to be all right. And it was, for another six years and through five operations to remove Steve's ever-growing tumor.

With the knowledge that there was no cure for this type of cancer, Brenda and Steve had to face up to life as best they could. That was when a friend advised them to see me.

I first saw them within two months of Steve's diagnosis. "I was nervous," Brenda says. "I did not know what to expect. Steve was a bit skeptical, but he humored me and came along. When I walked through Nancy's door for the first time, I had never experienced such a feeling of peace."

Steve survived many hardships as he moved through the maze of hospitals, doctors, and nurses. "A key person in keeping our life on an even keel all that time was Nancy," Brenda says. "She brought a wonderful calmness to Steve. She taught him to meditate—he had never done anything like that before. He seemed to take everything she taught him and make it his own. He was fascinated with beginning to understand his internal feelings and thoughts. He worked at being able to guide his emotional well-being to that place of peace. He loved the healing music that she used and bought some for himself to listen to in his long car rides to and from work. He kept going to his job up until two months before he passed.

"After we visited Nancy, we would sit in our car outside her home and reflect on what we had both learned. He wanted to hold on to that peace and sense of calmness as long as he could. It was a nightmare situation we were in. She couldn't cure him, but she made an incredible difference in how he coped with his illness. Nancy changed him.

"I was there for the first healing session. Steve was on the healing table and I was by his side, with my hands on his tumor. When Nancy started her work, there was such a powerful burst of energy that I collapsed. I was completely out cold on the floor. Later, Steve was very amused. He said, 'I am the patient, not you!'"

Back at the Dana-Farber Cancer Institute, through all his surgeries, his doctors were amazed at just how calm and collected Steve was. Little did they know, he brought his meditation practice with him and used it throughout the stressful situations he had to face. It may sound clichéd, but it is true: It's not what you get in life—it's what you do with what you are given.

He used to bring Brenda a fresh rose every week. After he died, Brenda had him cremated and brought some of his ashes to spread out in the ocean. Just as she let the ashes go, a perfect rose floated past her. She knows that it was Steve sending her his last rose.

CHAPTER

7

HEALING MEDITATIONS

Many people shy away from the idea of meditation. They think that sitting there, doing nothing, can't really be good for you. Nothing could be further from the truth. Five minutes of meditation will make a space in your mind that will allow you to think more clearly. It is from being in the present moment that we can actually move into the next moment with clarity.

Meditation gives people a chance to become familiar with their thoughts. I always tell my clients that our thoughts are so powerful that if we don't work with them and train them, it will be like getting into a ring with a sumo wrestler. My thoughts will wrestle me to the ground in no time flat, every time, unless I have trained through meditation.

Meditation brings me back to that still place within where I know we are all deeply connected to all living creatures in the universe. Meditation gives me a chance to turn my brain off, open my heart center, and listen from a place of connection, from a place of deep peace. Meditation is the time that I spend in stillness so that I can hear the answers to my heart's questions. The quiet time helps me to access an inner wisdom that is always available when I stop to pay attention. Nature is a great conduit for me. I can see divinity in the sunshine, the moonshine, and in the light in the eyes of other living beings. I hear God in the sounds of the morning songbirds, the stillness of the dawn, and I can definitely smell grace in the salty sea air.

I have been practicing prayer and meditation as well as teaching it for many years. For me, prayer is asking for guidance, and meditation is listening for the answers. I teach my clients that they can use prayer and meditation anywhere, anytime.

I begin every day with a prayer to be shown what to do throughout the day, and I end every day with a prayer of gratitude for the gifts I have received. Throughout the day I try to remember to stop whenever I'm afraid, worried, or confused and ask for help from God—you can call it anything that rings true for you.

For me, prayer is a conversation with something greater than myself. It gives me time to be in connection with something greater than anything I could ever imagine, something that my five senses can't define. Meditation is being mindful and paying attention to what is happening in the very moment that I am in. I believe that all of my meditations come from something greater than myself. Sometimes words are coming out of my mouth and I think, "Where are these ideas coming from?"

I teach healing meditations to my clients so that they can calm themselves down. One of the first forms of meditation I teach is mindfulness: paying attention to the sensations in your body at any given moment. It is amazing what the body is doing while our minds shift us from the past to the future, and the future to the past, seldom settling down into the present moment unless something very intense is going on.

It is in the present moment that your mind will begin to rest, slow down, and let go. As your mind chatter begins to slow down, your body can begin to rest, your central nervous system slows down, and your immune system can begin to work more efficiently.

Take a moment now to begin to settle down and try the miracle of meditation. Remember that there is no right or wrong way to do these healing meditations. However you move through them is perfect. I invite you to let go of self-judgment and criticism for a few moments. You can start practicing for as little as five minutes at a time.

Please make sure that you are comfortable, whether that means sitting in a chair or lying down flat. Very often, because of my back pain, I lie down to meditate. If you doze off, that's okay too. Sleeping is not meditating, but it must be what your body needs in that moment. Many meditation practices are too rigid for me. For example, some teachers insist that you sit in a certain way. Since these are healing meditations, it is important to be comfortable so that your body can relax into them.

In the beginning, invite yourself to practice for a few moments. With time, you will want to meditate longer. Please remember that whenever you are completely engaged in the moment that you are in, that moment is meditative. One pointed focus will bring you into the present moment. There are many ways to engage in meditation. You can do it while you are walking, running, biking, swimming, or doing the dishes.

Very often, when we begin to slow our bodies down, our thoughts become shy and disappear. They very quickly return as the meditation continues. The same thoughts repeat over and over in our brains, creating smooth, well-worn grooves. Often, there are just a few thoughts that return over and over again. As soon as we have escorted them out the front door of our mind, they scoot around and there they are again coming in through the back door. By gently noticing our thoughts without judgment or criticism, we can lovingly redirect those thoughts back to the present moment.

MEDITATION #1

The Withdrawal of the Senses

Let's begin to slow down and notice what is going on around you, what is going on inside of you at this moment. Begin by noticing your breathing. Feel your chest rise and fall with each breath in and each breath out. Notice your abdomen rising and falling as it, too, moves with your breathing. Notice the air coming in through your nostrils. Perhaps it feels a bit cool; perhaps it is a bit warmer as it moves out through your nostrils. Begin to listen to the sound of your breathing. Perhaps you can even hear the sound of your heartbeat. When thoughts come up from the past and the future, very gently let them go and bring yourself back into this moment. Right here and right now.

Imagine that you can begin to draw your eyes inward and downward toward the center of your chest. This is your heart center. I believe this is the single most important place in our bodies, because it is where we give and receive unconditional love. As you draw your eyes inward and downward toward this place in the center of your chest, imagine that you can see a space that is wide open and full of light, a place where there are no walls or doors or divisions. In this place everything is possible; there is a sense of freedom and spaciousness. Invite yourself to rest in this place, feeling safe, nurtured, supported, and greatly loved exactly as you are.

As you begin to rest in this place of acceptance and forgiveness, remember who you are. Remember your kindness, your compassion, your generosity, your humor, and your innate wisdom. Remember your courage, your strength, and your creativity. Remember that you are indeed greatly loved exactly as you are by something much greater than you could ever imagine. Feel your body as it begins to soften and open. Feel your mind as it continues to calm down. Notice that your thoughts are spreading out, and that there is even a little space between one thought and the next. It is in these spaces that I invite you to rest. It is in these great pauses of life that you find peace.

As you draw your eyes inward and downward, notice the stillness behind your eyes, and invite your brow to unfurl as you let go of fears, doubts, and worries. Invite your jaws to release and let go as your tongue expands on your lower palate, releasing any unspoken words. Just for a few moments, let go of any unspoken conversations from the past and the future, inviting your mouth to rest in a place of stillness. Imagine that your shoulders are dropping down away from your ears, as your shoulder muscles lengthen and let go. Bring your attention to your heart center and imagine that there is clear sparkling energy pouring in through your heart center, filling your physical body with health, wholeness, and vitality.

Feel yourself resting in this moment, right here, right now. In this moment there is no place to go, nothing to do, no one to see. In your heart center remember that in this moment, all is well.

And then when you are ready, very gently come back to the present moment as you begin to move your fingers and toes. Notice the difference you feel in your body and mind as you come out of this place of gentle relaxation.

Meditation gives your brain a chance to rest, and as your mind rests, your body is able to rest. For me, it is an essential tool for healing the body, mind, and spirit. The practice that I described above refers to the fifth limb of yoga, which entails drawing all of your organs of perception inward, away from the distractions of the external world. We do this so that we can better understand the innermost sensations, thoughts, and feelings. It is called *pratyahara* in the yogic tradition. I very often bring my clients to this place of deep peace so that they can rest.

MEDITATION #2

Create Your Own Healing Potion

I often use this meditation with my clients who are struggling with cancer.

Begin to settle down into this moment. Imagine that you can draw your eyes and ears inward and downward toward that still point within. Feel your shoulders drop away from your ears, and imagine that your neck muscles are lengthening from top to bottom, spreading from front to back and side to side.

Begin to pay attention to your breathing. Feel your chest rise and fall as you breathe in and out. Feel your abdomen expanding and contracting as you inhale and exhale. Feel yourself slowing down.

Bring yourself back into the present moment when your thoughts start to wander into the past or the future. Gently and courageously bringing yourself back to this moment. Invite yourself to let go of any judgment or self-criticism for a few moments. Remember that there is no right or wrong way to do any of these meditations.

Now, imagine a crystal bowl. You can make this crystal bowl any shape or size. Fill this crystal bowl with clear, liquid silk.

Next, pick your favorite color. A color that makes you feel wonderful from the inside out. A color that you would take a bath in. Once you have chosen this color, very gently swirl it into the liquid silk in your crystal bowl.

Choose your favorite sound. It could be a sound from nature, or a piece of your favorite music. It could be the sound of a loved one's voice. Imagine that you could swirl this sound into the liquid silk in your crystal bowl.

Pick one of your favorite scents. Again, this could be a scent from nature, the scent of a loved one's skin, or the smell of your favorite food cooking. Once you have identified this scent, swirl it into your healing potion in the crystal bowl.

The next thing to choose is your favorite taste. Something that you would choose to eat over and over again. If you were alone on a deserted island, what would you want to have with you to eat? Swirl this taste into your healing potion.

The last thing that we are going to add to your liquid silk is the emotion of unconditional love. We are going to very gently stir this all together, creating a healing potion just for you.

Now pick a beautiful sponge from the sea. Dip this sponge into your healing potion and swish it around, and very gently take your sponge and wring it out just a little bit. Imagine that you could bring this sponge inside of your body to the area that most needs healing.

We spend much time taking care of the outside of our physical bodies—we brush our teeth, wash our hair, clean our skin, and cut our nails. However, we spend very little time taking care of the insides of our bodies. Today, we are going to take our sponges, filled with our healing potion, and we are going to bring that sponge inside your body. Begin to energetically bathe, soothe, and heal that area of your body.

Imagine that you can encircle this area of your body, around and around with your healing potion. See this area of your body being washed with unconditional love. Watch as sorrow, sadness, grief, and fear all begin to melt away as they come into contact with unconditional love.

Watch as bruises, tears, rips, and scars begin to repair themselves when they come in contact with the most powerful force in the universe. Continue washing and bathing and soothing this area. See new healthy cells growing and multiplying in this area of your body. Watch them as they grow into a large mass spreading in all directions.

When you are through bathing this area, in your mind's eye, take the sponge out of your body and place it in the crystal bowl. This crystal bowl will now be taken by healing hands and recycled back into the universe in a positive manner. Now take a moment to look at all the hard work you have done by energetically clearing, cleansing, and healing yourself. See clear, healthy, vital, cells growing where there were none. See the darkness and toxicity evaporating and disappearing. See yourself as healthy, whole, and completely alive. Feel the freedom and spaciousness inside of you.

Now it is time to rest after all of that hard work. Rest your brain. Rest your eyes. Rest your voice. Rest your heart center. Rest your body. Rest your spirit.

MEDITATION #3

Body Scan Filled with Gratitude

Take a moment now to slow down. Find a comfortable spot to either sit or lie down. We are going to visit a few spots in the body where we habitually hold tension.

The first place that we are going to is the space behind your eyes. You may notice a little bit of tightness or tingling there. Very gently, shift your consciousness down to your jaws, left and right. You might feel a little bit of heat there. Notice your throat, and see if there might be a little bit of a lump there. If you swallow deeply once or twice, you might notice that you can release some of the energy in your throat.

Now bring your attention to the center of your chest. There might be a little bit of aching or pulling. Notice the energy in your abdomen. It might feel a little bit fluttery or tight. Shift your attention to the palms of your hands and the soles of your feet, and notice the warmth and tingling coming from them. These are all areas in our body where we habitually hold tension.

Gently close your eyes and imagine that you are resting in a place that is safe, full of acceptance, and forgiveness. Bring your consciousness down to your toes, starting with the big toes on your left and right feet.

Spread your consciousness out to the rest of your toes. You might feel a slight tingling when you bring your consciousness to certain parts of your body. Bring gratitude to your toes for all of the hard work they do for you. Without them it would be very difficult to stand up and balance.

Bring your attention now to the soles of your feet, especially the arches of your feet, and feel the sensations there. Notice that you have inside and outside edges on your feet. Take a moment to feel the tops of your feet, the insides and outsides of your ankles. Bring gratitude to both of your feet. Think of all the places that they have taken you. Think of all the things that they have done for you. Without them, it would be hard to run, walk, dance, jump, hop, skip, ride a bike, or swim.

As you continue to draw gratitude all the way up from your ankles to your knees, notice the sensations from your calves and your knees—the inside and outside edges of your knees, the fronts and the backs of your knees. Marvel at the way your knees bend, allowing you to sit, squat, twist, and turn.

Continue to pull gratitude up through your thighs—inside and outside edges, front and back, all the way up into your hips. Take a moment to be grateful for your hips, and all of the things that they do for you. Bring your attention to your right hip and your left hip. Feel your pelvic bone connecting your two hips, and notice how your lower back is gently expanding and softening.

Now bring your attention up to your torso, through your abdomen. Be grateful for your stomach and all of the hard work that it has done for you over the years. Bring gratitude to all of your organs—your liver, your digestive system, and your organs of reproduction. All of these body parts have helped you enormously over the years. Take a moment to be thankful for them.

Very gently shift your attention up to your heart. Be grateful for the tremendous work that it has done for you since before you were born. Feel your lungs in the center of your chest. Feel grateful for all they have done for you for many years.

Feel your spinal cord, running from your tailbone all the way up to the base of your skull. Feel each and every vertebra expanding and softening from back to front and side to side.

Be grateful for all your bones. Feel this gratitude moving out to your shoulders as they drop down away from your ears. Extend this gratitude from your shoulders all the way to your elbows, from your elbows to your wrists, from your wrists all the way to the tips of your fingers.

Feel your hands. Think of all the things that they have done for you in the last hour. Remember the miracle of your hands, wrists, elbows, and shoulders.

Very gently shift your attention up toward your head. Feel the sensations of your mouth, lips, teeth, tongue, and jaws. Be grateful for all that they do for you. Bring gratitude up to your nose, eyes, ears, face, forehead, and hair. Think of how well they served you. Notice these body parts.

Fill yourself with gratitude and the magic and beauty of how well your body works. Shift your attention to your brain. Notice the sensations inside your skull. Imagine that your brain is expanding and opening. Be grateful for the ability to think.

Bring softness and unconditional love to your entire body, your skin, your bones, and your blood. Marvel at all of the bits and pieces that make you uniquely you.

Now check in with those places where we habitually hold tension, and notice the softness and ease that now surround them. Feel the softness behind your eyes, the loosening of your jaws and mouth, the openness in your throat, the spaciousness in the center of your chest, the freedom in your abdomen. Feel the lightness in your hands and feet. Feel the gentleness, caring, and gratitude surrounding your amazing body.

Rest your body. Rest your mind. All is well.

MEDITATION #4
Eating Meditation

Recently, I did an eating meditation with my meditation class. I made two strawberry rhubarb pies and brought them to class in my double pie basket that I've had since my early twenties.

I started the class by passing out plates, napkins, and teaspoons of assorted colors. We took a few moments to marvel at these inventions, taking time to look at the shapes, sizes, and textures of these eating utensils. I then took the pies, to the delight of my students, out of the pie basket and passed them around for observation. How did the pies smell? What did they look like? How heavy were they? What physical sensations were experienced as we passed around the pies?

I then proceeded to tell them that we were not going to eat the pies for at least a half hour. We placed them in the middle of the table and began to settle into the moment.

* * *

Begin to slow down. Gently observe where your thoughts are leading you. Are you thinking about those pies? Is your mouth watering? How does your stomach feel? We then began to ponder all the ingredients that went into making these pies. We started with the rhubarb. In my garden, rhubarb is one of the first plants to come up in the early spring. It looks like small crimson red fists coming out of the earth. Those are the beginnings of the enormous leaves that will appear as the spring unfolds. Rhubarb grows so fast that it feels like I can watch it grow with my naked eyes. Eventually, the leaves look like green elephant ears attached to reddish-pink stalks that look like celery—the stalks are the edible part of the plant (the leaves are poisonous). Rhubarb is extremely tart, which is why it is often paired with strawberries and sugar.

Let's turn our attention now to strawberries. They also make an appearance in early spring. They grow low to the ground and spread by putting out runners from plant to plant. The flowers on the plants are white or pink, and the fruit begins to grow when the petals fall off. The fruit starts as a tiny green dot, which then grows into a small white strawberry, and finally into a bright red berry covered in tiny, crunchy seeds. It smells incredibly sweet.

Here is a story that represents mindfully eating a strawberry in the present moment:

> A young woman was walking through the forest when all of a sudden she heard a rustling in the trees behind her. She turned to look and saw an ambush of tigers coming toward her. She started running through the forest and out through a clearing that came to an abrupt end at a cliff. She looked back and saw the tigers moving in on her. She started to climb down the cliff

and managed to tuck herself under an overhanging branch that she held on to with one hand. She looked up and saw the tigers above and decided to plot her way down the cliff. All of a sudden, she saw another ambush of tigers coming around the corner below her. She looked up—tigers above; she looked down—tigers below. Then her eyes turned toward the branch she was hanging on to and she caught sight of a small strawberry plant with one perfectly red strawberry. Once more she looked up—tigers above. She looked down—tigers below. Then she reached up with her free hand and picked the strawberry and placed it in her mouth. She felt the juiciness and texture of the strawberry in her mouth. She heard the crunchiness of the seeds. She felt the coolness of the strawberry sliding down her throat. It was the most magnificent strawberry she had ever tasted.

Isn't life just like that? There are always tigers chasing us—the trick is to find those strawberries in the present moment.

Finally, the meditation students pick up their forks, carefully scooping up a small bite of the pie. We notice how the pie feels in our mouths, taking time to chew thoroughly before we swallow that first bite. We then savor the texture and taste as we feel it slide down the backs of our throats. Next, we put our forks down and feel the sensations in our bodies.

It takes us fifteen minutes to eat the whole piece of pie. It is truly miraculous!

Afterword

Many of the people I have worked with over the years have recovered from their cancer. Many have extended their lives. Some have moved into their deaths peacefully partly because I have been able to share with them what happened to me. They have all healed on some level, be it physical, emotional, or spiritual in nature.

But I don't want anyone to come to me and expect that I can physically heal them. Sometimes this does happen; however, I am really leading people to a space where healing is available to them—body, mind, or spirit. This is a still point within where they can rest. It is in this place of stillness that all the answers lie for each individual.

I can be joyful about someone's passing, whereas for most of their loved ones, it's a very painful or sorrowful experience. When patients come to see me, I can be excited for them because I know where they are going. I've told them all that when I get there, I want a big welcome home party!

When I did my very first healing, I knew that I would be doing this for the rest of my life. I said to myself, "This is right for me, and this is what I will be doing with the gift I was given." Up until that point, I had no idea what I was supposed to do with it. This is the way that I have been able to express it, and it is a tremendous gift for me to be able to help other people. When I worked on my first client, I said, "Okay, God, you can take me now. I've done a good job!"

The same goes with the book. When I first started working on it, I said to my editor, Noel, "Even if we help one person, then we've done a great job."

I pray daily to be of service to and through the vast energy that I call God. I am incredibly grateful that I get a chance to help.

We all have the ability to be of service; our lifetimes here are about awakening to our gifts and remembering who we are: our generosity, creativity, humor, compassion, kindness, and our unconditional love.

I do believe that giving and receiving unconditional love is our primary purpose here. We get a chance to do that every day in our own unique way.

After the awakening, it took me many years to integrate the whole thing and really commit to being here in physical form on the earth. In the early years, I remember going to the rabbi several times and telling him that I was yearning to go back to that light. It wasn't that I didn't love my life and the people in it. I did. It was just that the draw to go "home" to that light was enormous. I knew in my heart that it wasn't my time to leave, and yet the yearning was overpowering.

I knew then, as I know now, that I still have some more things to do here. One of those things was to write down all of my experiences and put it out there to help others. I hope with all my heart that I have helped you.

Acknowledgments

I would like to thank my original editor, Ernest Noel Young, for encouraging, prodding, and pulling this story out of me with great humor, patience, kindness, and open-mindedness. He never once doubted my sincerity. I know that much of what I told him was a stretch for him, and yet he continued to listen with an open heart. I will be forever grateful to him for helping me put my experiences into form and verse.

Additionally, I want to thank Trisha Thompson for her expertise, patience, and good humor. Small Batch Books was an excellent choice to bring my book into physical form.

Great, great gratitude goes out to my supportive and loving family. I am so grateful to my mother and father, Lloyd and Joyce, for giving me the gift of life in a big Jewish family, which has meant everything to me. Thanks to my sister, Lynnie, chanteuse extraordinaire, who has been a second mother to my children—sooo much fun to have our own Auntie Mame; to my brother, Andy, whose intense sense of clarity, intelligence, and quick wit has faithfully guided me through my life; and to my spirit sister Joni, whose incredible imagination and creativity is all-giving. I am forever grateful to Alice, who imparted her deep spirituality directly into my heart. Thanks also to my extended family: I adore you all!

To my three living angels: Patty, you are the best friend I could ever imagine; Angie and Judy, your love and enormous generosity have helped me become a lady of dignity and grace.

I would also like to thank the many people who trusted me enough to come to me for healing. It has been an incredible privilege to sit in stillness with you. Without you, I would not be a healer.

My greatest strength comes from the subtle Divine Presence that surrounds and permeates my universe. Without this Presence, I would be nothing.

Nancy Torgove Clasby has been a pioneer practitioner of spirituality and healing since 1998. In addition to her private healing practice, she is a reiki, polarity, and craniosacral practitioner as well as an ARCB-certified reflexologist. She has helped hundreds overcome chronic and terminal illnesses, often leading her clients on a path of self-healing, whether physical, emotional, or spiritual in nature.

Nancy received a B.A. from Lesley University, in Cambridge, Massachusetts, in 1980, and spent many years as a teacher, focusing on children with special needs. Her prior work includes recordings of guided healing meditations, and she is a sought-after meditation teacher.

Nancy lives in a small Massachusetts town on the Atlantic Ocean with two white fluffy cats and a brown dog, surrounded by lots of family and lifelong friends. She loves to ride her pink bike, swim in the ocean, knit, and bake pies. But mostly she loves to be with her family.

You can download Nancy's CD, *Healing Meditations with Nancy Torgove Clasby*, on iTunes.

And please visit her website: nancyclasbyhealingandmeditation.com.

CPSIA information can be obtained at www.ICGtesting.com
Printed in the USA
BVOW08s2258260916

463393BV00001B/13/P